"As true heir of Old Princeton,  has borne the torch of Reformed like no other North American s own faculty over two approaches ʋ ɔɔɪιpιure—Christocentric and Christotelic, respectively—called forth this book. With compelling appeal to Vos and Machen, and with succinct hermeneutical statements by current faculty, the authors rearticulate what Christocentric interpretation means and will continue to mean at Westminster."

—ROBERT W. YARBROUGH, Professor of New Testament,
    Covenant Theological Seminary

"I am happy to recommend this book because, as a Westminster Theological Seminary student in the 1970s, I was so excited about what I was learning that I could hardly wait to get to my classes. Especially wonderful were classes that showed the amazing unity of the Bible when understood in a system of Christ-centered biblical interpretation. That is the same system of interpretation that is taught at Westminster today and is affirmed so clearly in this book. I am also glad to see that this book clearly explains and rejects alternative approaches that deny the complete truthfulness of Scripture and that are inconsistent with the legacy of faithful commitment to Scripture that has marked Westminster Theological Seminary since its founding."

—WAYNE GRUDEM, Research Professor of Theology
    and Biblical Studies, Phoenix Seminary

"The organism of divine Christ-centered verbal revelation that we know as the Bible is both more deeply encultured and more profoundly transcultural then any of us ever grasps; but Westminster Theological Seminary has always led the pack in this quest, and still does, as the present book shows. It is very much on the right lines."

—J. I. PACKER, Board of Governors' Professor of Theology,
    Regent College

"At its founding in 1929, Westminster Theological Seminary dedicated itself to upholding the authority of the inerrant Word of God and to training its students to study the Bible confessionally and covenantally. Over eighty-five years later, it is a delight to see several senior members of Westminster's faculty unapologetically reaffirming these core commitments. . . . Whether you are new to the study of the Scripture or a seasoned reader of the Bible, *Seeing Christ in All of Scripture* will help you become a more thoughtful and careful student of the Old and New Testaments."

—GUY PRENTISS WATERS, James M. Baird, Jr. Professor of
New Testament, Reformed Theological Seminary, Jackson

"Ours is an age rife with relativism and self-absorption. How refreshing, then, to read a book like this that makes the case for saying that God's Word is coherent, its truth consistent, and that it is the means by which we stand addressed by God. But the authors do more. They also develop the principles by which we should understand this Word. Even though it was given over many centuries, its primary author, God, always had in view the incarnation and death of Christ. Christ is at the center of this revelation. This is what Westminster has always stood for, sometimes against great odds, and it is most commendable that this is being reaffirmed today so clearly and convincingly."

—DAVID F. WELLS, Distinguished Senior Research Professor,
Gordon-Conwell Theological Seminary

"What a delight to read this simple (but not simplistic) book on how to interpret the scriptures from members of the Westminster faculty. We are reminded of a fundamental principle of biblical interpretation: the scriptures are the word of God. . . . Warmly commended."

—THOMAS R. SCHREINER, James Buchanan Harrison Professor of
New Testament Interpretation and Professor of Biblical Theology
and Associate Dean of the School of Theology, The Southern
Baptist Theological Seminary

"This is the clearest, most concise, and most compelling case for the Christ-centered interpretation of all Scripture. Since the day Machen opened the door, Westminster has produced generations of pastors and teachers who faithfully and persuasively proclaim the gospel of Jesus Christ. These essays by Westminster's current scholars tell us that Machen's legacy is in good hands."

—STEPHEN J. NICHOLS, President, Reformation Bible College; Chief Academic Officer, Ligonier Ministries

"Studying biblical theology at Westminster Theological Seminary was a life-shaping experience for me. The professors there helped me see the deep structure of Scripture, in which every passage in each testament communicates the gospel of Jesus Christ. This has brought joy to my Christian experience and spiritual vitality to my ministry, as I expect this book from the same school will do for many readers today."

—PHILIP GRAHAM RYKEN, President, Wheaton College

"Every text has a context. That's not just for verses in chapters or chapters in books, but books within the context of the Bible. This book, by some of the most respected scholars in the world, rightly argues that the context of every biblical verse is the scriptural witness to Jesus Christ and his gospel. I commend this fine work to anyone who preaches or teaches or studies the Bible."

—RUSSELL MOORE, President, Southern Baptist Ethics & Religious Liberty Commission

"This is as clear a statement of the 'Westminster way' of reading Scripture of which I am aware. Anyone who wonders what Westminster Theological Seminary is all about would do well to consult this interdisciplinary commentary on Christ-centered biblical hermeneutics."

—KEVIN J. VANHOOZER, Research Professor of Systematic Theology, Trinity Evangelical Divinity School

"*Seeing Christ in All of Scripture* is a gratifying and encouraging book. Gratifying in that it testifies to the continued commitment on the part of Westminster Theological Seminary to the historic Reformed doctrine of Scripture and a method of interpretation that corresponds to this doctrine. Encouraging in that it promises a perpetuation of the vision of 'old Princeton' and J. Gresham Machen, founder of the seminary."

—CORNELIS VENEMA, Professor of Doctrinal Studies and President,
Mid-America Reformed Seminary

"I found this collection of essays on hermeneutics to be vital, as it emphasizes the necessity of 'an organic Christ-centered interpretation of Scripture.' In line with J. Gresham Machen's standpoint, Westminster Theological Seminary's current biblical scholars and theologians provide us with the highest view of Scripture, along with Christocentric understandings of redemptive history. This masterful work is a testimony to Westminster's integrity, and it deserves to be used as an excellent text for hermeneutics classes."

—BENYAMIN F. INTAN, President, International Reformed
Evangelical Seminary, Jakarta, Indonesia

"Historically, Reformed seminaries in Europe—Geneva, Edinburgh, and Leiden—have been at the forefront of formulating and defending not only the doctrine of Scripture, but also proper hermeneutical and exegetical methods. In the New World, Westminster Theological Seminary has now taken the lead. What is the relationship between Christ (the governing principle of Scripture) and a verse-by-verse study of the Bible? This volume of essays by four major biblical scholars teaches us how to provide this question with an orthodox answer and yet remain open to scholarly discussion. I heartily recommend it to all students of biblical interpretation."

—THOMAS SCHIRRMACHER, President, Martin Bucer
Theological Seminary; Chair of the Theological Commission,
World Evangelical Alliance

"This book is a succinct affirmation of the unity, progressive unfolding, and Christ-centered character of the Old and New Testaments. The four articles interact effectively with contemporary efforts to modify unqualified commitment to the written form of the Bible."

—O. PALMER ROBERTSON, Director, African Bible University of
Uganda; author, *The Christ of the Covenants*

"Westminster has been a distinctive champion in defending the faith and developing biblical principles and methods of hermeneutics in conformity with biblical teaching at the cost of possible sacrifice. In this book, the contributors, preeminent scholars in the area of biblical hermeneutics from Westminster Theological Seminary, present to the world the clearest and most legitimate guide of biblical principles and methods for interpreting the Bible. Hence, this book will be most beneficial to theologians, pastors, theological students, and all serious believers who desire to stand firm on the authority of the Bible and interpret the Bible accurately."

—IN WHAN KIM, President, Daeshin University and Seminary

"Westminster Theological Seminary has long taught and emphasized that Christ is the main theme of all Scripture. Recently, however, there has been controversy there over how he is the theme, especially of the Old Testament. I confess that this controversy has confused me. But *Seeing Christ in All of Scripture: Hermeneutics at Westminster Theological Seminary* has been a real help. It is certainly the clearest writing in the controversy so far, and it expresses very well the position that the seminary came to embrace. I'm hoping that it will get a wide readership."

—JOHN M. FRAME, J. D. Trimble Professor of Systematic Theology
and Philosophy, Reformed Theological Seminary, Orlando

"Westminster Theological Seminary has been heroic in their defence not only of the Scriptures as the inspired, infallible, inerrant word of God, but also in their approach to understanding and interpreting the Bible in a manner that doesn't betray this commitment. . . . In this book we have several penetrating essays from established scholars in their field who pioneer the way forward for sound biblical interpretation."

—MARK JONES, Senior Minister, Faith Vancouver Presbyterian Church, Vancouver

"What this book does is set out in a superb way the basic hermeneutical principles that must underlie a Reformed evangelical approach to Scripture. For over seventy years Westminster was known for a unified approach to Scripture by all its faculty. After the more recent disputes, this book reaffirms with delightful clarity how we are to approach the interpretation of inspired Scripture, and in particular where Westminster stands on these issues. Peter Lillback introduces the book, and Vern Poythress, Iain Duguid, Greg Beale, and Richard Gaffin have contributed outstanding chapters that are going to serve a wide readership. They have brought the discussion down to a level that will ensure many Christian readers will grasp what is at stake, and find the content of this book sets out principles that will help direct their study of the Scriptures. This book, notable for both its clear exposition of the subject and its concise discussion, needs extensive distribution and use."

—ALLAN M. HARMAN, Research Professor, Presbyterian Theological College

"Perhaps no other issue facing the church today carries with it pitfalls and trajectories for error and for damage to the Bride of Christ than that of faulty biblical interpretation. Westminster Theological Seminary has a glorious track record of pulling us back again and again to the essential components of biblical hermeneutics. In our day the seminary has brought together biblical scholars and teachers with a heart for the glory of Christ in their interpretation of the Scriptures. Here in one place you will find a safe guide to the riches of the Bible's witness to Christ in all the Scriptures. I commend it highly and urge it upon all who have a heart to know God and His Christ."

—LIAM GOLIGHER, Senior Minister, Tenth Presbyterian Church, Philadelphia

"*Seeing Christ in All of Scripture* nicely captures how the Westminster faculty handles the Bible. As a God-Authored whole, Scripture reveals the saving, exalted Christ. He comes to us, 'clothed' in these words. . . . Deep orthodoxy and profound commitment to the written Word continue to make Westminster a blessed place to train for ministry."

—HOWARD GRIFFITH, Associate Professor of Systematic Theology and Academic Dean, Reformed Theological Seminary, Washington DC

"In view of the recent controversy surrounding hermeneutics at the seminary, it is refreshing to hear that the Board, faculty, and student body are recommitting themselves to the historic orthodox and Reformed doctrine of Scripture, its method of interpretation, and its implications for the life of the church. The essays in this volume are a welcome reaffirmation of the *modus operandi* of that tradition which was embodied in the first generation of the seminary. The words of Machen's essay in this volume reverberates in each of the essays so that the message of the self-attesting Christ of Scripture cannot be missed as the foundation of the seminary's service to Christ's glorious church. As an easily accessible volume, pastors and laity will greatly benefit from the instruction and the edification of the authors in this work."

—WILLIAM D. DENNISON, Professor of Interdisciplinary Studies, Covenant College

"For generations, the faculty of Westminster Theological Seminary has called for scholars, pastors, and lay people alike to see Christ throughout Scripture. This volume sketches approaches to

Christ-centered biblical interpretation that remain true to the full authority of the Scriptures and to the lordship of Christ over all."

—RICHARD L. PRATT JR., President, Third Millennium Ministries

"In John Calvin's typical style of 'clarity and brevity,' the authors of this book reaffirm what Westminster Theological Seminary stands for. They draw connections, open perspectives, and invite consideration and discussion. Toward the five hundredth anniversary of the rediscovery of 'sola Scriptura,' these four articles not only demonstrate the connection between Luther's theses and Westminster's theology, but also offer essential contributions to the present discussion on hermeneutics."

—HERMAN J. SELDERHUIS, Professor of Church History, Theological University Apeldoorn, The Netherlands; Director, Refo500

"In a day when biblical scholars and theologians obstruct the view of many in the pew, this book removes the obstacles so that the towering figure of Jesus Christ clearly emerges from the pages of Scripture. This book is brief and un-technical but rich in terms of its theological significance for understanding that Jesus Christ stands at the center of redemptive history and the Scriptures. Anyone interested in learning what it means that all of Scripture speaks of Christ should consult this little book."

—J. V. FESKO, Professor of Systematic and Historical Theology and Academic Dean, Westminster Seminary California

"Writings on hermeneutics are ironically notorious for often being convoluted and obscure. Only after many twists and turns does one emerge with relief from a labyrinth. Not so this little book, which has the merits of brevity and clarity that make it a joy to read. Striking here is not the current insistence on the Bible as an ancient and all too human text, or the challenge for today's reader to find a cipher to make it mean something, but commitment to respect the text for what it is. This means taking the dual authorship of Scripture seriously, which alone allows mining the treasures of Christ that bring knowledge of salvation and incentive for proclamation, so serving the *solas* of a reformational heritage."

—**PAUL WELLS**, Emeritus Professor, Faculté Jean Calvin

"The four essays in this small volume do more than declare the position of Westminster Theological Seminary in Philadelphia; they also succinctly and clearly promote the historic Reformed and covenantal understanding of how Scriptures (and especially the OT in relation to the NT) are to be interpreted. These essays—for their conciseness and clarity—will prove to be an excellent introduction to biblical interpretation."

—**T. DAVID GORDON**, Professor of Religion and Greek,
   Grove City College

"That Christ is both the center and goal of the Old Testament is a distinctive perspective which Westminster greatly underscores. This is drawn from Scriptural attestation that Christ is the last spoken word of God which encompasses God's spoken word in the Old Testament past. . . . The representative scholars in this great work have left no one in doubt about their collective determination to bequeath a legacy of faithful and distinctive scholarship to their successors. I wholly recommend this work to all."

—**PHILIP TACHIN**, Lecturer, National Open University
   of Nigeria, Lagos

"Reformed theology helps us see the gospel and read the Bible more faithfully. These brief essays help suggest ways in which our confession might better enable us in both tasks."

—**MICHAEL ALLEN**, Associate Professor of Systematic and
   Historical Theology, Reformed Theological Seminary

"Were the Christological prophecies and anticipations, which Jesus, and the New Testament in general, saw in the Old Testament, planted there by God, with the human authors having some notion of what was involved? Or were they the retrojection of a later age, whether or not God had some role in that later perception? The first option affirms God's inspiration as the source of the teaching of both Old and New Testaments. The second option drifts away from the immediate role of God in the writing of Scriptures towards a more Deist notion of the action of God in the world. This work concisely outlines the understanding of inspiration, interpretation and kindred subjects, which allows us to affirm that Jesus' interpretation of the Old Testament was in accord with the original plan of God."

—NOEL WEEKS, Senior Lecturer in Ancient History and Associate of the Department of Classics and Ancient History, University of Sydney

"It is a privilege to commend *Seeing Christ in all of Scripture*. This volume not only affirms the continued integrity and excellence of theological education at Westminster, it also pointedly highlights Westminster's leadership in the propagation of biblical theology, solid biblical exegesis, and confessional integrity."

—HARRY REEDER, Senior Pastor, Briarwood Presbyterian Church, Birmingham

"This small book was forged out of the recent controversy over Scripture and hermeneutics at Westminster Theological Seminary. Written clearly and with minimal jargon, it can be read in one sitting—but don't be deceived, for it is bursting with rich insights. Lillback and his A-team have effectively given us a short theological meditation on Luke 24, one that clarifies what Christocentric reading of the Bible means for Machen's Seminary and the Old Princeton tradition that it represents. I recommend the book highly."

—HANS MADUEME, Assistant Professor of Theological Studies, Covenant College

"These essays set forth what is entailed in Christ-centered biblical interpretation that seeks to be ever mindful that God is Scripture's primary Author. They do so with a clarity born of painful controversy. . . . Brief though they are, these pieces sketch out sound principles for exploring both the profound unity and the variety of God's inerrant Word."

—DENNIS E. JOHNSON, Professor of Practical Theology, Westminster Seminary California; author, *Him We Proclaim: Preaching Christ from All the Scriptures* and *Walking with Jesus through His Word: Discovering Christ in All the Scriptures*

"A depth of riches. That's what Westminster is as an institution. And that's what comes through in the pages of this brief but significant book."

—NANCY GUTHRIE, author, Seeing Jesus in the Old Testament series

"The authors of this short study present clearly and comprehensively the main aspects of sound biblical interpretation. . . . By emphasizing the interdependency of biblical and systematic theology, they argue convincingly that Jesus Christ is not only the goal of Old Testament revelation, but the center of the Bible's entire redemptive message. Written within the particular context of Westminster Theological Seminary, this book is a gift to the Church universal."

—PIERRE BERTHOUD, Emeritus Professor, Faculté Jean Calvin

"At a time when the trustworthiness and relevance of God's Word continues to be minimized, I am thankful for the faithful ministry of Westminster Theological Seminary. Through this important new book, these eminent scholars have provided not only a clear description of Christ-centered interpretation, but also its compelling and life-changing nature. This is a book that is timely, accessible, and edifying."

—JULIUS J. KIM, Dean of Students and Professor of Practical Theology, Westminster Seminary California

SEEING CHRIST IN ALL OF SCRIPTURE

SEEING CHRIST IN ALL OF SCRIPTURE

Hermeneutics at Westminster Theological Seminary

Edited by Peter A. Lillback with contributions from Vern S. Poythress, Iain M. Duguid, G. K. Beale, and Richard B. Gaffin Jr.

WESTMINSTER
SEMINARY PRESS
Philadelphia, Pennsylvania

In memory of the founding faculty

May Westminster Theological Seminary always remain
suaviter in modo, fortiter in re

"The genuine believer takes the whole of Scripture as a living organism produced by the Holy Spirit to present Christ to him. On every page of Scripture, he finds traits and traces of the Mediator."
—GEERHARDUS VOS, *Reformed Dogmatics*

"Jesus was the Messiah because he fulfilled what had been spoken concerning Him in the Old Testament. He was the very One of whom the prophets spake. He came into this world for the explicit purpose of fulfilling what they had written concerning Him."
—E. J. YOUNG, *The Study of Old Testament Theology Today*

"The Old Testament follows God's one great plan for human history and redemption, and the plan is not only from him, but centers on him: his presence in his incarnate Son. . . . The witness of the Scriptures to Christ is the reason they were written—and of him and through him and to him are all things (Rom 11:36)."
—EDMUND CLOWNEY, *Preaching Christ in All of Scripture*

"God seeks spontaneous and loving acceptance of his Word. As he wanted this in paradise, so he wants it now. Christians must be, like the Apostle Paul, all things to all men in order to save some. Firm and insistent in their ultimate objective, they must approach their goal *suaviter in modo*."
—CORNELIUS VAN TIL, *A Christian Theory of Knowledge*

CONTENTS

————◈————

ACKNOWLEDGMENTS

———✦———

This book is the product of many faithful laborers at Westminster Theological Seminary. I am grateful to Vern, Iain, Greg, and Dick for contributing their fine essays. I am also grateful to James Baird, Chris Carter, Ben Dahlvang, Charles Williams, and the rest working with Westminster Seminary Press for their management of this project and creative input. Thanks are due to our editors: Rick Matt, Mary Ruth Murdoch, and Stephanie Taylor. A special "thank you" is in order for Amanda Martin at P&R Publishing for her gracious consultation. Finally, I would like to thank the donors, without whose support this book would not be a reality.

—PETER A. LILLBACK
President
Westminster Theological Seminary

INTRODUCTION

———✛———

PETER A. LILLBACK

Dr. J. Gresham Machen established Westminster Theological Seminary to produce "specialists in the Bible" who would preach and teach "the whole counsel of God." Following Machen's lead, Westminster has historically stood for the truth of Scripture. One dimension of this commitment is that Westminster teaches its students to preach Christ from the entire Bible—from both the Old Testament and the New Testament.

In order to fulfill its founding vision, Westminster's faculty members, throughout the seminary's history, have taken an "*ex animo*" vow, that is, a sincere, heartfelt commitment, to the Westminster Standards. These confessional documents, the Westminster Confession of Faith and the Larger and Shorter Catechisms, are held as the best expression of the system of biblical truth—"the whole counsel of God"—thus far developed in the church of our Lord Jesus Christ. It is from these documents that the seminary takes its name.

This introduction calls attention to the consistency of biblical interpretation that exists today at Westminster Theological Seminary. The harmony among the theological disciplines at Westminster is due to a shared method of interpreting Scripture, a shared *hermeneutic*, that is drawn from Westminster's confessional standards. Although expressed in distinctive ways, Westminster's hermeneutic remains cohesive and compatible throughout the theological curriculum. It is my privilege, then, to introduce this collection of brief essays written by four of Westminster's leading scholars. Herein, you will find a witness to the hermeneutical unity at Westminster through the perspectives of Dr. Vern Poythress, Dr. Iain Duguid, Dr.

Greg Beale, and Dr. Richard Gaffin Their reflections span the whole of Scripture and express the deep continuity that courses through the diverse fields of biblical interpretation at Westminster Theological Seminary.

In chapter 1, Dr. Poythress, professor of New Testament interpretation, draws our attention to how the concept of covenant bears on the work of hermeneutics, reaffirming the perspective of Westminster's founding professor Cornelius Van Til:

> Cornelius Van Til was right in teaching that there is an antithesis in principle between the thinking of Christians and non-Christians, covenant keepers and covenant breakers. Presuppositions—one's basic commitments—make a difference in how one approaches any subject. . . . One always has to think through what difference the antithesis Van Til speaks of makes in the arena of hermeneutics.
>
> First, there is a difference particularly when we consider the interpretation of Scripture. Christians should treat the Bible in harmony with its actual character: it is the Word of God. Non-Christians do not share this commitment. This makes a difference because we must pay attention to the intention of the author if we are to interpret his work correctly. The Bible has human authors, of course, but its main author is God himself.

In chapter 2, Dr. Duguid, professor of Old Testament, offers four basic principles of Old Testament interpretation that belong not just to scholars, but that are truly accessible to the general Bible reader:

> The Old Testament is not primarily a book about ancient history or culture, though it contains many things that are

historical and that describe ancient cultures. Centrally, the Old Testament is a book about Christ, and more specifically, about his sufferings and the glories that will follow—that is, it is a book about the promise of a coming Messiah through whose sufferings God will establish his glorious, eternal kingdom. To say this is simply to repeat what Jesus told the discouraged disciples on the road to Emmaus.

In chapter 3, Dr. Beale, professor of New Testament and biblical theology, defines and summarizes some of the pivotal principles for hermeneutics, with a focus on New Testament interpretation:

New Testament scholars generally affirm that a text cannot mean what it never could have meant to its original author or his readers. This principle, however, is not absolute since biblical authors did not have exhaustive knowledge of what they wrote. Only God has exhaustive knowledge, which is not contradictory to the human author's knowledge but an organic expansion of it. This is especially apparent when one recognizes that Old Testament prophecies and narratives are understood with greater clarity (but not in a contradictory way) in the light of Christ's coming and the revelatory events connected with the new covenant age.

In chapter 4, Dr. Gaffin, emeritus professor of biblical and systematic theology, explains the importance of hermeneutics for all the theological disciplines at Westminster, especially systematic theology:

Systematic theology at Westminster Theological Seminary is radically nonspeculative. This is so in the sense that the distinguishing concern of systematic theology is to provide a presentation of the unified teaching of Scripture as a whole.

Accordingly, its very existence depends upon sound biblical interpretation. As systematic theology is a comprehensive statement of what "is either expressly set down in Scripture, or by good and necessary consequence may be deduced from Scripture" (Westminster Confession of Faith 1.6), exegesis is its lifeblood.

The compatible perspectives represented by these four authors have not always been encountered consistently at Westminster Theological Seminary. In the last decade, a hermeneutical dispute arose over the role of Christ in the Old and New Testaments. Essentially, two diverse theologies of Scripture contended for the faculty's allegiance. One placed Christ at the organic center of the entire Bible's redemptive message, while the other merely located Christ as the goal of Old Testament revelation. Resolving that controversy solidified a cohesive view of the role of Christ in Westminster's hermeneutic, a view that reflects the profound words of Dr. Gaffin: "Christ is the mediatorial Lord and Savior of redemptive history not only at its end but also from beginning to end. He is not only its omega but also its alpha, and he is and can be its omega only as he is its alpha."[1] Thus, this little work is presented to the public as an introduction to the hermeneutical method that today characterizes the biblical scholarship of the Westminster faculty.

Reformed scholars have always affirmed the centrality of Christ for understanding the message of the whole Bible; they have not done so without biblical precedent. As our Lord and Savior, Jesus Christ, says in John 5:46–47: "For if you believed Moses, you would believe

---

1. This quote is from appendix C, "Biblical Theology at Westminster Theological Seminary," originally published on World Reformed Fellowship, June 30, 2014; http://westm.in /1ROGwYs. See also the "Affirmations and Denials Regarding Recent Issues," republished as appendix B, for Westminster's official position on the recent controversies over hermeneutics (adopted by the Board of Trustees December 3, 2008).

me; for he wrote of me. But if you do not believe his writings, how will you believe my words?" Following the teaching of Jesus, our Reformed forefathers interpreted many passages as portraying Christ as the heart and goal of biblical revelation.[2] The Christ-centered manner in which the Reformed hermeneutical method engaged Scripture developed out of the unifying principle of the covenant. The essence of covenant theology was well captured in the climax of the Reformation's confessional compositions, namely, the Westminster Standards. Chapter 7 of the Westminster Confession of Faith addresses the relevance of the covenant for biblical interpretation:

> 3. Man, by his fall, having made himself incapable of life by that covenant, the Lord was pleased to make a second, commonly called the covenant of grace; wherein he freely offereth unto sinners life and salvation by Jesus Christ; requiring of them faith in him, that they may be saved, and promising to give unto all those that are ordained unto eternal life his Holy Spirit, to make them willing, and able to believe.
>
> 5. This covenant was differently administered in the time of the law, and in the time of the gospel: under the law, it was administered by promises, prophecies, sacrifices, circumcision, the paschal lamb, and other types and ordinances delivered to the people of the Jews, all foresignifying Christ to come; which were, for that time, sufficient and efficacious, through the operation of the Spirit, to instruct and build up the elect in faith in the promised Messiah, by whom they had full remission of sins, and eternal salvation; and is called the Old Testament.
>
> 6. Under the gospel, when Christ, the substance, was exhib-

---

2. See, for example, Gen 3:15; 15:6; Deut 18:15;Ps 22:30; 32:1–2, 5; Isa 9:5–6; 42:1; 53:10; 55:4–5, 6; Jer 31:33–34; Ezek 36:26–27; Luke 2:32; John 6:37, 44–45; 8:56; Acts 2:29–36;3:20, 22; Rom 4:11, 16–24; 10:6–10; 1 Cor 10:1–4; Col 1:13; 2:11–12; Gal 3:7–9, 10; 1 Pet 1:19–20; Heb 4:2; 8–10; 11:13.

ited, the ordinances in which this covenant is dispensed are the
preaching of the Word, and the administration of the sacra-
ments of baptism and the Lord's Supper: which, though fewer
in number, and administered with more simplicity, and less
outward glory, yet, in them, it is held forth in more fullness,
evidence, and spiritual efficacy, to all nations, both Jews and
Gentiles; and is called the New Testament. There are not therefore two covenants of grace, differing in substance, but one
and the same, under various dispensations.

These classic Reformed emphases on the covenantal unity of the
Bible highlight the necessity of an organic Christ-centered interpretation of Scripture. All of Westminster Theological Seminary's faculty
and board members have committed to this confessional hermeneutic since the seminary's founding. The seminary today continues to
believe that the hermeneutical method identified in the Reformational tradition of Westminster is biblically sound and in fact essential for a high view of Scripture in an age of doubt, controversy, and
compromise.

By holding fast to the traditional Reformed hermeneutical
method, Westminster Theological Seminary has sought to remain
faithful to the stirring speech that Dr. Machen presented to the seminary community as the school opened on September 25, 1929,
in Philadelphia. Machen declared the following in his inaugural
address:

We believe, first, that the Christian religion, as set forth in
the Confession of Faith of the Presbyterian Church, is true;
we believe, second, that the Christian religion welcomes and
is capable of scholarly defense; and we believe, third, that the
Christian religion should be proclaimed without fear or favor,
and in clear opposition to whatever opposes it, whether from

within or without the church, as the only way of salvation for lost mankind. On that platform, brethren, we stand. Pray that we may be enabled by God's grace to stand firm. Pray that the students who go forth from Westminster Theological Seminary may know Christ as their own Savior and may proclaim to others the gospel of his love.[3]

As you read the following chapters, we invite you to join us in the historic and lofty calling of Westminster Theological Seminary to train specialists in the Bible who will proclaim the whole counsel of God, from the whole of Scripture, for Christ and his kingdom.

Please pray that our students may "know Christ as their own Savior and may proclaim to others the gospel of his love." After all, that is what seeing Christ in all of Scripture is all about.

---

3. This quote is from appendix A, "Westminster Theological Seminary: Its Plan and Purpose," which previously appeared in J. Gresham Machen, *What is Christianity? And Other Addresses*, ed. Ned Bernard Stonehouse (Grand Rapids: Eerdmans, 1951), 224–233.

Recommended Reading From Peter A. Lillback

"'The Infallible Rule of Interpreting Scripture': The Hermeneutical Crisis and the Westminster Standards." In *Resurrection and Eschatology: Theology in Service of the Church: Essays in Honor of Richard B. Gaffin Jr.*, edited by Lane G. Tipton and Jeffrey C. Waddington, 283–339. Phillipsburg, NJ: P&R, 2008.

Thy Word Is Still Truth: Essential Writings on the Doctrine of Scripture from the Reformation to Today. Edited by Peter A. Lillback and Richard B. Gaffin Jr. Phillipsburg, NJ: P&R, 2013.

1

Biblical Hermeneutics

VERN S. POYTHRESS

Biblical hermeneutics has played an important role in nearly all the teaching I have done over the years at Westminster Theological Seminary. My desire is to train students to interpret the Bible faithfully, so I am continually dealing with the interplay between broader principles of interpretation and particular texts. Every year I teach an MDiv-level course called "Biblical Hermeneutics: Old and New Testaments." That means I am always thinking about and discussing hermeneutics; it is a background framework when I am considering a particular passage of Scripture.

Presuppositions for Hermeneutics

Cornelius Van Til was right in teaching that there is an antithesis in principle between the thinking of Christians and non-Christians, covenant keepers and covenant breakers. Presuppositions—one's basic commitments—make a difference in how one approaches any subject. Van Til's principles have had a big influence on my work in hermeneutics. One always has to think through what difference the antithesis Van Til speaks of makes in the arena of hermeneutics.

First, there is a difference particularly when we consider the interpretation of Scripture. Christians should treat the Bible in harmony with its actual character: it is the Word of God. Non-Christians do not share this commitment. This makes a difference because we must pay attention to the intention of the author if we are to interpret his work correctly. The Bible has human authors, of course, but its main author is God himself.

This thinking about authorship provides us with a good start in working through the distinctiveness of biblical hermeneutics. But there is more to it than that. Christian presuppositions and the work of regeneration make a difference in principle in *every* sphere of life, not merely on the central question of the authorship and authority of Scripture. So we must think through how we should differ from the world in our view of truth, our view of meaning, our view of history, our view of language, and so on. The Bible requires a "special" hermeneutic because it is a special book, the Word of God. But by its instruction the Bible should also transform our ideas about *general hermeneutics*, that is, the issues concerning interpretation of non-inspired human writings.

Based on Christian presuppositions, we engage in transforming the very idea of what texts are and what interpreting texts means. All texts whatsoever live and move and have their being in the presence of God, the God of truth and power and beauty. Does that imply that we can learn nothing from non-Christians? Van Til emphasized not only antithesis, but also *common grace*. Unbelievers have many truthful insights in spite of their corrupt hearts. But the challenges for evangelicals are mostly in the other direction. Evangelical scholars are disposed to use hermeneutical procedures originally developed on the basis of non-Christian presuppositions. They make minimal changes to these procedures, of course, to avoid directly denying the possibility of miracles or the divine authority of Scripture. But minimal changes are not enough. We ought to be rethinking the entire process of interpretation on the basis of sound presuppositions.

Hermeneutical Circularity?

When people hear about using the Bible to transform our ideas about hermeneutics, it can be disturbing to some of them. The process sounds circular. The circle begins with the Bible. We use the Bible to derive hermeneutical principles. Then we use hermeneutics to interpret the Bible. And so our interpretation of the Bible depends on itself! How can we be sure that we have it right? To make the process more complicated, we can add a third stage to the circle, namely, systematic theology. We use the Bible as our source for systematic theology, which is supposed to be a summary of what the Bible teaches. Then we use systematic theology as a presupposition for hermeneutics. And then hermeneutics guides how we interpret the Bible. In this process, we never leave behind our initial use of the Bible, which might be flawed.

Instead of this picture, some people would prefer not a circle but a line. They advise us first to establish sound hermeneutical principles. Then interpret the Bible. Then form a systematic theology. Only in this way can you be sure of your foundations and be sure that you are not departing from a flawed starting point.

Ah, but it is not so simple. There is no way to form sound hermeneutical principles in a vacuum, apart from religious commitments. You are either for God or against him. And even if you are for him, you need growth and sanctification. You are not perfectly pure, your mind is not perfectly pure, and your hermeneutical preferences are not perfectly sound. That is the nature of life in a fallen world.

Therefore, we praise God for his provision. He has sent Christ precisely for the purpose of rescuing us out of this fallen world:

> He has delivered us from the domain of darkness and transferred us to the kingdom of his beloved Son, in whom we have redemption, the forgiveness of sins. (Col 1:13–14)

As one aspect of this redemption, he has given us the Scriptures for our purification:

Sanctify them in the truth; *your word* is truth. (John 17:17)

Thus, we need the Bible as the guide to enable us to transform and purify our hermeneutical principles. The circle from the Bible to systematic theology to hermeneutics to the Bible is not a vicious circle, but a spiral of growth and progress, guided by the work of the Holy Spirit in illumination.

Does the dynamism of growth imply that everything is uncertain? A postmodern skepticism might tempt us to draw a veil of uncertainty over everything and to bolster the idea of uncertainty with the label "humility." But here again the Scriptures offer a useful corrective. The Bible says that its central message is clear and that God has in fact designed his Word with skill. Scripture helps those who begin in darkness by leading them into the light:

The testimony of the LORD is sure, making wise the *simple*.
(Ps 19:7)

Your word is a lamp to my feet and a light to my path.
(Ps 119:105)

But the path of the righteous is like the light of dawn,
which shines brighter and brighter until full day.
(Prov 4:18)

Again Jesus spoke to them, saying, "I am the light of the
world. Whoever follows me will not walk in darkness,
but will have *the light of life*." (John 8:12)

I have come into the world as light, so that whoever believes in me may not remain in darkness. (John 12:46)

Human Authors

Let us consider one area of discussion in hermeneutics: how do we analyze the human authors? The presuppositions of the world will tell us that the human authors of the Bible were merely men of their times. How could they be otherwise? So, interpretation must proceed wholly by fitting those authors into their social and historical environments. Anything else is alleged to be a denial of history or a denial of humanity.

But the authors of Scripture received the aid of the Holy Spirit. Through the working of the Holy Spirit, they inwardly wanted to do whatever God wished to do. And the Spirit is God himself, who is the source of infinite creativity. His presence and his special work in inspiration do not make human beings less than human. Rather, he transforms sinful humanity toward humanity as God originally designed it. More than that, the authors' humanity is transformed into the image of Christ, who is the perfect man, the last Adam. This transformation took place in a measure even in the Old Testament, because the Holy Spirit even then was the same Holy Spirit who is one with the Father and the Son. He acted in mercy and grace toward human beings on the basis of the atonement that Christ was yet to accomplish in the future.

This presence of the Holy Spirit has implications. If an interpreter tries to eliminate the presence of God through the Holy Spirit, he might claim that an Old Testament passage merely reflects its Ancient Near Eastern environment and a human author caught in that environment, an environment that itself is purely human, without the presence of God.

But that kind of reading is certainly wrong. God is sovereign over the Ancient Near Eastern environment, along with all other environments. He reveals himself in general revelation through all environments, so interaction is natural between what God says and the environment in which he says it. This natural interaction extends also to the human authors whom God raised up to be the bearers of his Word. As we observed, the Holy Spirit did not transform these men into that which was less than humanity; rather, he moved them in the direction of the fullness of humanity as God intended it to be. But that fullness of humanity is not something that we can equate with our most prosaic pictures of flat and one-dimensional communication.

In the end, communication through the inspiration of the Holy Spirit is uncontrollable by mechanical calculation. We will know humanity fully only at the end of the process of our *own* transformation, when we will be conformed to the image of Christ (2 Cor 3:18).

The Part and the Whole

Another issue that arises with regard to hermeneutics is the relation of each part of the Bible to the whole. God caused the Bible to be written over a period of more than a thousand years. As Lord of history and Lord of revelation, he spoke "at many times and in many ways" through the prophets (Heb 1:1). Theologians call this process "progressive revelation." God did not say everything at once. The earlier communications take into account the limitations in the understanding of people at earlier times. The later communications build on the earlier. What is implicit in the earlier often becomes explicit in the later. The climax to this process of revelation comes in Christ: "in these last days he has spoken to us by his Son, whom he appointed the heir of all things, through whom also he created the world" (Heb 1:2).

Taken together, these communications from God have a marvelous unity centered on the divine purpose of redemption and re-creation. Yet there is also a lot of diversity—diversity of human authors, diversity of genres, diversity of stages in redemptive history, and diversity between the comparatively small beginnings and the climactic ending. How do we handle this unity in diversity and diversity in unity?

We can start with some simple principles. God is one God. He is consistent with himself. So the earlier and the later harmonize, as do the poetic song and the historical narrative and the proverb and the prophetic vision. At the same time, God as Lord of redemption and Lord of history unfolds his purposes gradually, and we need to listen respectfully to the intentionally sparse communications at earlier points.

Communication has depth. A single human speaker can unpack an opening statement further on in his speech and provide illumination that gives new depth to its meaning. Even human communication is not always one-dimensionally flat and shallow. Human writing can suggest depths or allude to implications without spelling them out. Or it can spell out these matters in additional communication, perhaps at a later time or in a sequel. How much more so when it comes to divine communication!

So no simple formula is going to provide all the answers to interpreting divine communication at earlier and later times. The most basic principle is the principle of knowing God. God is deep, infinitely deep. Is he also inaccessible? No. God made us and has come to us to save us in Christ. His words are therefore accessible through the mediation of Christ in the power of the Holy Spirit—the Spirit of Christ whom the ascended Jesus has poured out on his people (Acts 2:33). Knowing God is truly the path of "the light of dawn, which shines brighter and brighter until full day" (Prov 4:18). Or, as Jesus says, "I am *the way*, and *the truth*, and the life; no one comes to the Father except through me" (John 14:6).

Recommended Reading From Vern S. Poythress

God-Centered Biblical Interpretation. Phillipsburg, NJ: P&R, 1999.
In the Beginning Was the Word: Language—A God-Centered Approach. Wheaton, IL: Crossway, 2009.
Inerrancy and Worldview: Answering Modern Challenges to the Bible. Wheaton, IL: Crossway, 2012.
"Dispensing with Merely Human Meaning: Gains and Losses From Focusing on the Human Author, Illustrated by Zephaniah 1:2–3." *Journal of the Evangelical Theological Society* 57, no. 3 (2014): 481–99.
Reading the Word of God in the Presence of God: A Handbook for Biblical Interpretation. Wheaton, IL: Crossway, 2016.

2

Old Testament Hermeneutics

IAIN M. DUGUID

The interpretation of the Old Testament is sometimes presented as a complex affair, a task only to be attempted by those with advanced degrees and a fluent understanding of Ancient Near Eastern culture, intertestamental literature, and ancient languages. To be sure, each of these areas of study can be a great asset to our understanding of the Word of God, but in this short essay I want to suggest four basic principles for interpreting the Old Testament that can be grasped and applied thoughtfully by almost anyone who approaches this part of the Scriptures.

I. The Center of the Old Testament Is Christ

The Old Testament is not primarily a book about ancient history or culture, though it contains many things that are historical and that describe ancient cultures. Centrally, the Old Testament is a book about Christ, and more specifically, about his sufferings and the glories that will follow—that is, it is a book about the promise of a coming Messiah through whose sufferings God will establish his glorious, eternal kingdom. To say this is simply to repeat what Jesus told the discouraged disciples on the road to Emmaus:

And he said to them, "O foolish ones, and slow of heart to believe all that the prophets have spoken! Was it not necessary that the Christ should suffer these things and enter into his glory?" And beginning with Moses and all the Prophets, he interpreted to them in all the Scriptures the things concerning himself. (Luke 24:25–27)

This is the same message that Jesus gave to all of his followers during his forty-day master class on Old Testament interpretation, delivered between his resurrection and his ascension:

Then he said to them, "These are my words that I spoke to you while I was still with you, that everything written about me in the Law of Moses and the Prophets and the Psalms must be fulfilled." Then he opened their minds to understand the Scriptures, and said to them, "Thus it is written, that the Christ should suffer and on the third day rise from the dead, and that repentance and forgiveness of sins should be proclaimed in his name to all nations, beginning from Jerusalem." (Luke 24:44–47)

This understanding of the Old Testament was the consistent message of the preaching of the apostles. So, for example, Paul told King Agrippa:

I stand here testifying both to small and great, saying nothing but what the prophets and Moses said would come to pass: that the Christ must suffer and that, by being the first to rise from the dead, he would proclaim light both to our people and to the Gentiles. (Acts 26:22b–23; cf. Acts 3:18, 21, 24; 17:2–3; 1 Pet 1:10–11)

Thus, when we interpret the Old Testament correctly, without allegory or artificial manipulation but in accordance with Jesus's own teaching, the central message on every page is Christ. That does not mean that every verse taken by itself contains a hidden allusion to Christ, but that the central thrust of every passage leads us in some way to the central message of the gospel.

II. The Old Testament Had a Message for its Original Hearers, Not Just for Us

This is an important complementary truth to the first principle. It is a mistake to read the Old Testament as if its Christ-centered message were only revealed to us, who read it through the lens of its fulfillment in him. Hebrews 1:1 tells us that God spoke in the past to his Old Testament people through his servants the prophets; he speaks now as well to us, climactically, through his Son. The Pentateuch spoke God's Word of challenge and promise to those who were about to enter the Promised Land in the days of Moses.[1] Isaiah spoke to those who lived in Judah in the days of Ahaz and Hezekiah, not only to those who read his prophecies about the Babylonian exile and about Christ after their fulfillment. The Book of Kings addressed the spiritual needs of those who found themselves wrenched away from the Promised Land because of their sins and the sins of their fathers. Ezekiel and the Chronicler wrote to discouraged believers in their own times who wondered about the value of any attempt to serve God in the aftermath of the exile.

This is not to say that the prophets never spoke of the future. On the contrary, they repeatedly predicted the future, sometimes in

---

1. See my article "Hagar the Egyptian: A Note on the Allure of Egypt in the Abraham Cycle," *Westminster Theological Journal* 56, no. 2 (Fall 1994): 419–21, for an example.

extravagantly precise detail (for example, Isa 44:28; Dan 11). Part of the Lord's claim to uniqueness among the gods of the Ancient Near East is the fact that he alone spoke the future accurately through his prophets (Isa 45:18–21; Amos 3:7).[2] Indeed, one of the scriptural tests of a prophet's authenticity is the fact that the words he speaks are fulfilled (Deut 18:22); such a test of course requires fulfilled predictions. Those predictions that came true in the short term were intended as encouragements to believe the promises of God that had not yet been fulfilled.

These first two principles lead us to make two further observations about interpreting the Old Testament.

III. The Old Testament Writers Did Not Fully Understand Everything about Which They Wrote

This reality is clear in a number of places in the Old Testament itself. Prophets like Daniel and Zechariah frequently did not completely grasp the visions that they were shown (see Dan 8:27; Zech 4:13). Indeed, it is hard to imagine how Daniel could have fully understood a prophecy like that in Daniel 11, which contains so many specific references to people and events during the period between Alexander the Great and Antiochus Epiphanes.[3] As Numbers 12:6–8 reminds us, prophecy by its very nature is often dark and obscure, unlike the Lord's clear word through Moses. In particular, some aspects of God's purposes in Christ necessarily remained veiled throughout the Old Testament period, only to be clarified through the coming of the Son.

---

2. Hence the repeated refrain, "Then you will know that I am the Lord." Fulfillment of the prophetic word attests the identity of Yahweh as well as that of his messengers.

3. According to John Goldingay, Daniel 11 refers in a specific, historically identifiable way to thirteen of the sixteen rulers of the Ptolemaic and Seleucid kingdoms between 322 and 163 BC. See Goldingay, *Daniel* (Word Biblical Commentary; Dallas: Word, 1989), 295–6.

One way to think about this is to imagine attending a "prophecy conference" in the year 10 BC. By then, the participants would have had the entire Old Testament, as well as several centuries of reflection on it during the intertestamental period. Yet if someone had presented a paper anticipating the crucifixion of the Messiah on the basis of Psalm 22, or his resurrection on the basis of Psalm 16, or even the virgin birth on the basis of Isaiah 7, some vigorous debate might have ensued. It was not obvious ahead of time that these prophecies should be interpreted in that way. However, with the benefit of hindsight, the New Testament authors rightly identified these texts as finding their anticipated fulfilment in Christ's life, death, and resurrection. It is not that the New Testament writers were creatively assigning new and alien meanings to these old texts. Rather, the force of Jesus's statement that it was "necessary that the Christ should suffer these things" (Luke 24:26) suggests that a proper reading of the Old Testament expectation of the messiah necessarily compelled them to recognize Jesus Christ as its true fulfillment. This is why Paul could argue from the Old Testament so convincingly in the context of Jewish evangelism.

IV. The Old Testament Writers Truly Understood Some Things They Described

For that reason, it is important not to overstress the ignorance of the divinely inspired prophets, as well as the other writers of the Old Testament. No one was in doubt as to the signification of Micah's prophecy of a coming ruler to be born in Bethlehem (Mic 5:2): when Herod asked the birthplace of the messiah the answer was unequivocal (Matt 2:5–6). When Jesus says that Abraham saw his day and rejoiced (John 8:58), he surely had in mind (at least) the events that transpired in Genesis 22. Abraham did not have a full understanding of the sufferings of Christ and the glories that would follow, perhaps, but he had a true understanding that just as the Lord had provided the ram to die in place of his beloved son, Isaac, so too the Lord would provide a substitute for Abraham's own sins. Daniel may not have grasped the exact details of the coming conflict between the Ptolemies and the Seleucids as described in Daniel 11; he did, however, recognize that the broad philosophy of history presented in that chapter provided a clear rebuke to his overly optimistic hope that, with the completion of the seventy years of judgment prophesied in Jeremiah, the end would soon be nigh (see Dan 9:2). Instead, before the end would come, there would continue to be wars and rumors of wars, with empires rising and falling, but when the dust finally settled, the triumph would belong to the saints of the Most High.

Likewise, whatever Daniel himself made of his vision in Daniel 7 of a human figure (a "son of man") who possessed uniquely divine attributes ("coming on the clouds"), the central meaning of that vision was clearly explained to him by the angel in 7:16–17. Daniel understood the central message that there would be continuing trials and sufferings for the saints before the final glories that would come only when God intervened to bring history to a close. It is precisely because of what he understood that Daniel was alarmed by the vision (7:28), as well as comforted by the promise of ultimate triumph through this mysterious "son of man."

Moreover, the content of these visions that the Old Testament saints correctly grasped is nothing less than the gospel itself, albeit in types and shadows. This is what Paul says in Galatians 3:8: "And the Scripture, foreseeing that God would justify the Gentiles by faith, preached the gospel beforehand to Abraham, saying, 'In you shall all nations be blessed.'" The gospel of the sufferings of Christ and the glories that would follow was clear to Old Testament readers from the earliest days, even if only in outline and sometimes obscure form. This is crucial to affirm, since the Old Testament saints were saved by faith in the gospel of Jesus Christ just as we are and not by some other method of salvation. In order to maintain that notion, it is necessary to affirm (as Paul does), that the gospel message was genuinely visible to the eyes of faith in the Old Testament long before its revelation in fullness in the coming of Christ.

In many ways, the situation of the Old Testament saints is not so different from our own as we live between the now and the not yet. We still see God's ultimate plan for the world through a glass darkly just as the believers in our hypothetical first century BC prophecy conference did. Like them, we know clearly and unmistakably some things about God's plans for the future. Christ will return bodily and triumph over all of his enemies (Ps 2). The kingdoms of this world must become the kingdom of our Lord and of his Christ (Rev 11:15). Whoever believes in Christ will never be abandoned by him (Heb 13:5). At the same time, there are many things about Christ's return that we know only vaguely; in some details we may be surprised to find our expectations proven wrong. Nonetheless, when we look back from the vantage point of fulfillment, our hearts, too, will burn, and we will judge ourselves foolish of heart and slow to believe all that God had revealed to us in his Word. In other words, our astonishment will not be because the fulfillment differed from the promise, or because some parts of the promise proved to be dead ends, but because we had not begun to grasp the height and depth of the wisdom of God that is at work for our salvation in Christ.

Many things that were concealed during the Old Testament period have now been revealed in the light of Christ's appearing. Some things will remain partially hidden from our eyes until the consummation. Nevertheless, the consistent and plain message of the gospel runs throughout every page of God's Word, from Genesis to Revelation. The Bible's message of the gospel repeatedly points the saints of all ages and generations back to the sufferings of Christ and the glories that will follow.

Recommended Reading From Iain M. Duguid

Living in the Gap Between Promise and Reality: The Gospel According to Abraham. Phillipsburg, NJ: P&R, 1999.

Living in the Grip of Relentless Grace: The Gospel According to Isaac and Jacob. Phillipsburg, NJ: P&R, 2002.

Living in the Light of Inextinguishable Hope: The Gospel According to Joseph. Phillipsburg, NJ: P&R, 2013.

Is Jesus in the Old Testament? Phillipsburg, NJ: P&R and Westminster Seminary Press, 2013.

3
New Testament Hermeneutics

G. K. BEALE

This brief essay offers some notes on the practice of hermeneutics and sets forth a collection of principles and presuppositions that should direct how we interpret particular biblical texts. Numerous books have been written on hermeneutics, so what follows will merely give an overview of the most essential guiding truths for biblical interpretation. While the focus will be on the New Testament, some discussion will include the Old Testament.

I. Biblical Exegesis

Biblical exegesis can be defined in the following way: the attempt to determine an author's meaning—and ultimately God's meaning, which is more exhaustive than that of the human author—in one particular passage through such means as the analysis of its genre (each genre—apocalyptic, poetry, narrative, epistles, etc.—has unique rules of interpretation), textual criticism, grammar, flow of ideas, historical background, word meaning, figures of speech, and relationship with other biblical passages through direct quotation or allusion. The greatest rule in doing biblical exegesis is that the immediate context of a passage is crucial in determining the meaning of that passage. There are also broader contexts that affect the meaning of a particular passage: (1) the book in which the passage appears; (2) the corpus to which the book belongs; and (3) the testament in which the book or corpus is located.

II. Validating a Biblical Interpretation

The following questions should be addressed in order to validate or show the probability of a proposed interpretation:

1. Does the interpretation fit well in the context of the passage?
2. Is the interpretive idea in harmony with the rest of biblical revelation and theology?
3. How well does the proposed interpretation illuminate the parts of the passage?
4. How does the proposed interpretation compare with competing interpretations offered by other commentators?

The best interpretation honors and incorporates the various details of the passage. If one interpretation seems to relate well to a paragraph of verses save one verse, and another interpretation makes good sense of all the verses, then the latter interpretation is better.

III. Divine Inspiration

The Protestant canon of the Old and New Testaments comprises the divinely inspired, authoritative material for doing biblical interpretation. Tradition (commentaries, sermons, etc.) can help us understand the Bible, but we must remember that tradition is not inspired and, therefore, not ultimately determinative of the Bible's meaning.

IV. Human Authorship

New Testament scholars generally affirm that a text cannot mean what it never could have meant to its original author or his readers. This principle, however, is not absolute since biblical authors did not have exhaustive knowledge of what they wrote. Only God has exhaustive knowledge, which is not contradictory to the human author's knowledge but an organic expansion of it. This is especially apparent when one recognizes that Old Testament prophecies and narratives are understood with greater clarity (but not in a contradictory way) in the light of Christ's coming and the revelatory events connected with the new covenant age.

V. Biblical Theology

One eminently important hermeneutical principle is that Scripture should be used to interpret other Scripture. This hermeneutical principle is often called the "analogy of Scripture." Passages in Scripture, especially unclear passages, are to be read in light of other passages that speak more clearly on the same topic or develop the same idea. The discipline of biblical theology builds on this hermeneutical principle as it studies each corpus of Scripture in its own right, especially with respect to the corpus's place in the redemptive-historical unfolding of God's revelation.[1] Accordingly, biblical theology is "the exhibition of the organic progress of supernatural revelation in its historic

---

1. See D. A. Carson, "Unity and Diversity in the New Testament: The Possibility of Systematic Theology," in *Scripture and Truth*, ed. D. A. Carson and John D. Woodbridge (Grand Rapids: Zondervan, 1983), 69.

continuity and multiformity."[2] This means that a biblical-theological approach to a particular biblical text seeks to give its interpretation in relation to its literary context, its redemptive-historical epoch, and to the epoch or epochs preceding and following it. By so doing, one can see more clearly the organic development of earlier Scripture in relation to later Scripture.

In this respect, all of Scripture is to be viewed as narrating a unified, true historical narrative about how history began (the commissioning of Adam to rule as a priest-king and prophet), how humanity fell (Adam's representative sin), and how humanity will be restored for the glory of God (ultimately climaxed with Christ's inaugurated latter-day redemption at the cross and resurrection, consummated with his final return) in a new cosmos. Thus, one must understand the beginning and middle of the biblical story in order to understand its climax and ending. Likewise, one must understand the ending in order better to understand the beginning.

VI. The New Testament Use of the Old Testament

One good way biblical theology can aid the interpretation of particular passages is by pointing us to how the New Testament interprets Old Testament passages. The interpretive presuppositions employed by the New Testament writers to understand the Old Testament serve as a guide for Christians interpreting the Old Testament.[3]

1. The New Testament writers assume corporate solidarity or representation. Corporate solidarity is the idea that

---

2. Geerhardus Vos, "The Idea of Biblical Theology as a Science and as a Theological Discipline," in *Redemptive History and Biblical Interpretation*, ed. Richard B. Gaffin Jr. (Phillipsburg, NJ: P&R, 1980), 15.

3. The following 5 presuppositions are drawn from G. K. Beale, *Handbook on the New Testament Use of the Old Testament* (Grand Rapids: Baker, 2012), 96–97.

an individual represents a group. The individual's actions and the resulting consequences apply to all persons in the relevant group, even though they did not perform the action of the individual. For example, Adam's disobedience and condemnation represented all humanity, so that humanity as a whole was seen as disobeying like Adam and therefore is condemned in him.

2. In the light of corporate solidarity or representation, the New Testament writers view Christ the Messiah as representing the true Israel of the Old Testament (e.g., Isa 49:3) and the church as the true Israel of the New Testament (cf. Gal 3:16 and 3:29).

3. The New Testament writers see history as unified by a wise and sovereign plan so that the earlier events are designed to correspond and point to the latter events (cf. Matt 5:17; 11:13; 13:16–17).

4. The New Testament writers believe that the age of eschatological fulfillment has come in Christ (cf., Gal 4:4; Heb 9:26).

5. As a consequence of the preceding presupposition, the New Testament writers hold that the latter parts of biblical history function as the broader context in which to interpret earlier parts because the various human authors all have the same, ultimate divine author inspiring them. One deduction from this premise is that Christ is both the goal toward which the Old Testament points and the end-time center of redemptive history, which is the key to interpreting the earlier portions of the Old Testament and its promises.[4]

---

4. Cf. 2 Cor 1:20; Matt 5:17; 13:11, 16–17; Luke 24:25–27, 32, 44–45; John 5:39; 20:9; Rom 10:4.

These presuppositions have profound interpretive implications. For example, the New Testament sees some Old Testament prophecies about Israel as being fulfilled in Christ and the church. This would be a wrong interpretation of these prophecies unless one understands the presupposition that Jesus sums up and represents true Israel, and that the church is also to be understood as true Israel in her union with Jesus (presupposition number 2 above). Or, recall the Old Testament prophecies of the Messiah, which the New Testament writers then see as fulfilled in the church. Again, if we understand the presupposition that Jesus the Messiah represents true Israel, then prophecies about him can be viewed as fulfilled in the church as true Israel. By itself, the second presupposition about Jesus as true Israel clears up what otherwise would be a number of problematic uses of the Old Testament.

Another example of a helpful presupposition is the notion that history is unified by a wise and sovereign plan, so that the earlier parts are designed to correspond and point to the latter parts (presupposition number 3 above). This explains why New Testament writers could see events from the Old Testament to be prophetic and fulfilled in Christ and the church (e.g., Hos 11:1 in Matt 2:15). Without this presupposition, such New Testament uses would appear to misunderstand Old Testament historical texts as prophecies.

VII. The Perspicuity of Scripture

The divine authorial intentions communicated through the human authors of Scripture are accessible to contemporary readers. Though no one can comprehend these intentions exhaustively, we can understand them sufficiently, especially for the purposes of salvation, sanctification (growth in faith, love, and hope), and the glorification of God. The Reformers argued for this understanding of the perspicuity or clarity of Scripture, rejecting medieval Catholicism's allegorical method of interpretation, which allowed interpreters to read their own meanings into Scripture.

The perspicuity of Scripture also contrasts the so-called post-modern evangelical view that one's presuppositions result in a distortion of the original meaning of a text so that interpreters can only come away with interpretative conclusions that reflect their own theological predispositions. A presupposition is like a lens of a pair of glasses. If the lens is green, then everything you see is green; if blue, then everything you see is blue. For example, Democrats are accused of reading into the Constitution too much social engineering and government control because that is their lens, while Republicans are accused of reading in too much capitalism and personal responsibility. Both are accused by the other of distorting the true meaning of the Constitution.

Rather than the postmodern view that denies readers the ability to access objective meaning in Scripture, a good biblical-theological assumption is that all interpreters have presuppositions and that some presuppositions distort the originally intended meanings of ancient texts, while other presuppositions actually guide one into the truth of texts. Keeping with the above illustration, there are some theologically colored lenses that cause one to see the true theological color of Scripture. The presuppositions of the biblical writers themselves as expressed in Scripture have the power through the Spirit to regrind the presuppositional lenses of those who read Scripture to lead them into the truth (cf. John 8:32 with John 14:6, 17; 15:26; 16:13; see also 1 John 5:20).[5]

---

5. E.g., E. D. Hirsch, *Validity in Interpretation* (New Haven: Yale University Press, 1967), and Kevin Vanhoozer, *Is There a Meaning in This Text?* (Grand Rapids: Zondervan, 1998), both of whom are optimistic about readers being able to discern sufficiently but not exhaustively authorial intentions of writers; for interaction with those who are skeptical, see Vanhoozer.

VIII. Divine Redemption

Redeemed interpreters are not perfect. They still suffer from the effects of the fall in their minds, bodies, and souls. Christians are being conformed to the image of Christ (Rom 8:29), but we are not yet perfected in Christ's image. Our interpretations, therefore, are also not yet perfect. This fact needs to be balanced out, however, by the doctrine of the perspicuity of Scripture: God has revealed clearly what is necessary for our salvation and sanctification, and for his glorification. This is why he inspired the human authors of the Bible to write. Thus, one does not need to be a scholar to understand the Bible's teaching on these topics. The effects of the fall on believing interpreters need to be understood, moreover, in light of the fact that believers have been regenerated. They have a new, better lens through which to understand the Bible, though they will not have a full understanding of Scripture until the end of the age and the final resurrection of the saints (1 Cor 13:12).

Acts 17:28 says "in him we live and move and have our being"(esv). This is true of us as interpreters of Scripture. God's sovereign preservation of our minds, bodies, spirits, and souls is crucial for us to interpret rightly. If we become unhealthy in any part of our being, it can affect our ability to interpret. Whenever we interpret rightly it is because of God's sovereign direction. In an ultimate sense, God directs every part of the interpretive process. If God's will has brought about the events narrated in Scripture and has superintended the biblical writers to record and interpret these events, we should also maintain that he guides our interpretation of Scripture. Scripture plainly says that God is sovereign over all things, and this must include our interpretation of Scripture. God's sovereignty over our interpretation, however, does not mean that God reveals interpretations to us magically by causing them to pop into our minds in response to our prayers for understanding. Rather, God's sovereignty means that we must depend on God's presence with us to guide us in the interpretive process. We are not neutral interpreters; instead, we should realize that God is accomplishing his will through our interpretation of the Bible. Does not Jesus say that "apart from me you can do nothing" (John 15:5; NASB)? Then this statement must cover the important task of interpreting Scripture.

It is also true that only because God anoints us with his Spirit are we able to learn his Word at all (1 John 2:27).[6] The Spirit gives us a new, regenerated mindset when we believe, and this mindset serves as a new lens through which we can increasingly understand God's Word as we grow in our faith under the Spirit's power (1 John 5:20; 1 Cor 2:10–15). Accordingly, those with the gift of teaching are especially enabled by the Spirit to persevere through the "reading" and "pains" of scriptural study and "to be absorbed in these things" (1 Tim 4:13–16; my translation). The Spirit gives them a desire and endurance to "labor in the word and teaching" (1 Tim 5:17; my translation) and to be a "workman . . . handling accurately the word of truth" (2 Tim 2:15; my translation). The same is more generally true to one degree or another for all Christians. God reveals himself and his truth through his Spirit in the Scriptures, making them God's "living oracles." And, since the words of the Bible are living, they can transform us (e.g., see Rom 12:2).

But the role of the Holy Spirit is not to whisper in our ears the meaning of a passage or to change the meaning of a passage to suit our own situation. The Spirit's work focuses on the application of the Bible's meaning to our lives, on guiding us in applying the meaning of a text to different situations. Isaiah 55:11 says, "so shall My word be which goes forth from My mouth; It shall not return to Me empty, Without accomplishing what I desire, And without

6. The substance of the preceding paragraph and up to this point has been influenced by Walter C. Kaiser and Moises Silva, *An Introduction to Biblical Hermeneutics* (Grand Rapids: Zondervan, 1994), 266–69.

succeeding in the matter for which I sent it"(NASB). Thus, the Spirit is the agent who accomplishes the goals God desires his Word to achieve, whether that be obedience, faithfulness, repentance, hardening, or judgment—and ultimately all these things are to work toward his own glory. Accordingly, the Spirit enables God's people to believe for salvation, to grow in sanctification, and to think and do that which glorifies God. God's inerrant written Word is the window through which we encounter his beautiful presence.

The Spirit's role is also to keep us humble, abolish our pride, and cause us to be open to the message of the Scriptures. If we want to please God and not ourselves, then we will not be threatened if Scripture presents to us a meaning that goes against one of our previously held theological or ethical views. The Holy Spirit leads us to love the true God, and thus to love what is true. This means that when God's Word presents to us an idea that goes against something that we have greatly valued, we love God's Word and acknowledge that our own ideas were wrong. The Spirit also convicts us when we are "foolish and slow of heart to believe" in what the Bible says (cf. Luke 24:25; my translation), thus enabling us to understand and to be receptive to what Scripture says (Luke 24:32, 45).[7]

IX. Hermeneutics for Contemporary Application

It is clear that some commands and examples set in Scripture are not to be followed in the way originally intended, as with the command not to boil a kid in its mother's milk (Exod 34:26) or the example of casting lots to choose church leaders (Acts 1:22–26). Christ fulfills many of the Old Testament laws (e.g., as partly expressed by Matt

---

7. I am grateful to John Piper, "The Goal of Exegesis and the Rationale for Finding Relationships between Propositions" (unpublished article), for some of the thoughts in this paragraph.

5:17 and Rom 10:4), so the way these are obeyed in the New Testament era must be understood in light of Christ. As this is a large area of discussion, this essay will not address such commands and examples from Scripture exhaustively. Offered here instead are some general guidelines with which to approach the question of application, especially from the New Testament perspective.

Some scholars contend that a New Testament command carries over to the present only when the situation is comparable to that to which the New Testament command was originally addressed. For example, some believe that the office of elder was created for churches where false teaching was a problem. Thus, this view would say that the office of elder (which excludes female candidates) is applicable only for churches throughout the church age that are affected by false teaching and not for other churches.

How could redemptive-historical considerations bear upon this issue? According to the New Testament, the latter days have been inaugurated with the first coming of Christ (e.g., Acts 2:17; 1 Cor 10:11; Gal 4:4; Heb 1:2; 9:26; 1 John 2:18) but will not be consummated until he comes at the end of the age (e.g., Heb 9:26–28; cf. 1 Pet 1:20 with 1:5). The ethical commands given to God's latter-day people will naturally remain valid for them until the period of the end times is concluded. Part of what this entails is that the latter-day tribulation has commenced with the coming of Jesus and the establishment of the church (e.g., 1 Tim 4:1 and 2 Tim 3:1, the contexts of which show that the end-time tribulation involving false teaching has begun but is not consummated; see likewise 2 Pet 3:3; Jude 18; 1 John 2:18). Accordingly, the end-time trial, including that of false teaching, is a condition that continues throughout the church age. This means that churches are either affected internally by false teaching or are threatened externally by it. Since the office of elder was created, at least in part, to guard the doctrine of the church, and if all churches are either affected or threatened by eschatological false doctrine, then there is no church situation throughout the church age that does not require the presence of elders.[8]

Another redemptive-historical consideration bears upon this issue of contemporary application. One way to describe believers collectively throughout the entire interadvent era is as those who are in the visible "church" and who profess to be "in Christ." Paul, for example, says that it is those in the "church" for whom his commands have ongoing validity. Such commands are not intended for only a particular church in a particular situation but for all "the churches" (1 Cor 4:17; 7:17; 11:16; 14:33–37; 1 Tim 3:15–16). The references to "the churches" in 1 Corinthians are not only to multiple house churches in Corinth but also to other churches in other regions (as is apparent from 1 Cor 4:17; 11:16; and 1 Tim 3:15–16). As long as there are churches and as long as there are people "in Christ," which is a condition enduring throughout the interadvent age, the commands to the "churches" and those "in Christ" are valid.

In the light of the interadvent age being a "latter-day" age of the "church" and all those who are "in Christ," the vast majority of the commandments given in the New Testament are valid because they are given to those living during this age. The burden of proof is on an interpreter to show that a command does not apply throughout the interadvent epoch, and this does occasionally occur.

There has also been debate about how to apply historical narratives to Christians today. Some believe that characters in these narratives are examples that we are to imitate. While there is some truth to this, it is a secondary consideration. In Old Testament narratives one should see what the segment is saying about God and then see how the characters in the narrative relate to the redemptive-historical

---

8. Christ, as Lord of the church, in his mediatorial office, appoints undershepherd elders as a continuation of the Old Testament office of elder (see Edmond P. Clowney, *The Church* [Downers Grove: InterVarsity, 1995], 206–12).

message about God. Only then can one perceive how the narrative relates to today and applies to us. For example, some want to copy Joseph as either an example of one who unconditionally loves his family or as someone who faithfully perseveres through trial. But, in fact, the main point of the narrative about Joseph is how God graciously preserves Israel by bringing his people into Egypt with the intent to bring them out again (cf. Gen 50:19–50). By first recognizing the narrative of God's preservation of Israel, one can properly understand that Joseph is an example to copy in his faithful perseverance in God's sovereign dealings (e.g., see Ps 105:16–22).

The same is the case in the historical narratives of the Gospels and Acts in the New Testament. One's first impulse should not be to emulate the characters in these narratives, but to see what the narratives teach about the person of Christ (in the Gospels) or the work of Christ's Spirit in causing the kingdom to expand (in Acts). Once one understands these main perspectives, then one will better understand what these narratives demand of their readers: first to trust in and worship Christ and his Spirit, and then, secondarily, to determine how these narratives work to encourage believers to emulate Christ. Acts, for example, typically portrays believers as following the cruciform pattern of Christ's life in the Gospels, a pattern believers today should follow.

Conclusion

In this short essay we have focused on the principles most crucial for proper interpretation of Scripture in accord with its divine purpose in Christ. As we have seen, the presuppositions that the Bible demands us to bring to the interpretive process help us to understand how all of Scripture is focused christologically.

Recommended Reading From G. K. Beale

The Erosion of Inerrancy in Evangelicalism: Responding to New Challenges to Biblical Authority. Wheaton: Crossway, 2008.

A New Testament Biblical Theology: The Unfolding of the Old Testament in the New. Grand Rapids: Baker, 2011.

Handbook on the New Testament Use of the Old Testament: Exegesis and Interpretation. Grand Rapids: Baker, 2012.

4

Systematic Theology and Hermeneutics

RICHARD B. GAFFIN JR.

Systematic theology at Westminster Theological Seminary is radically nonspeculative. This is so in the sense that the distinguishing concern of systematic theology is to provide a presentation of the unified teaching of Scripture as a whole. Accordingly, its very existence depends upon sound biblical interpretation. As systematic theology is a comprehensive statement of what "is either expressly set down in Scripture, or by good and necessary consequence may be deduced from Scripture" (Westminster Confession of Faith 1.6), exegesis is its lifeblood.

Plainly, then, systematic theology has a hermeneutical concern, no less than all the other theological disciplines.[1] Though this concern is not so formally explicit as in Old and New Testament studies, it ought to be alert to issues of exegetical method as well as to the wide range of principles and procedures that inform valid interpretation. Systematic theology, accordingly, does not have a "special" hermeneutic of its own but one it shares with all other theological disciplines.

---

1. At first glance, that may not appear to be the case for church history. But, as has been aptly observed, church history as a whole may be profitably considered, as much as anything, as the history of the interpretation of Scripture, particularly when "interpretation" is understood as the lived-out understanding (or misunderstanding, as the case may be) of Scripture.

The Bible is God's Word

The most basic consideration for biblical hermeneutics is this: the Bible is God's Word. In fact, this is better seen as a pre- or meta-hermeneutical consideration.

To be sure, the way in which this truth is brought to expression may be challenged; whether or not it can be said better, whether or not the doctrine of Scripture admits to a more adequate expression, remains an open question. This doctrine, like all doctrinal formulation, is hermeneutically qualified.

But the conviction expressed (or that ought to be expressed) in saying, "The Bible is God's Word," arises immediately from being exposed directly to Scripture—not only, perhaps not even primarily, to its explicit self-witness in passages like 2 Timothy 3:16 and 2 Peter 1:20–21, but also to Scripture throughout. This conviction, produced by the Holy Spirit, may not be called into question or made hermeneutically problematic.

To be clear about this conviction, certainly it does not exist in the abstract, apart from believing the truth of the gospel and trusting Christ; it is a normal component of saving faith. Still, while inseparable from accepting the central content of Scripture, it is, in distinction, a settled conviction about the *text* of Scripture, namely, that the words of the text are the words of God himself in a way that is unique, a way that, in terms of their origin, is not true of any other text. In form as well as content, in its wording as well as its subject matter, the Bible is God's Word.

This conviction about the text of Scripture is captured best and most succinctly by saying that God is "the author thereof" (Westminster Confession of Faith 1.4). This raises the issue, for one, of the role of Scripture's human authors, an issue to which we will return below. Here we may note, utilizing a classical distinction, that in relation to the human authors, God is the primary author of Scripture; the role of the former as authors is secondary. God, then, is not merely in back of the Bible and its origin in a general, loosely providential or indirect way. Rather, he is ultimately responsible for every word in the Bible with nothing less than full and proper authorial accountability. Put negatively, were the Bible to be in error, God, not just the human authors, would be chargeable with error.

The Unity of the Bible

Given, then, that Scripture is God's very own Word, the first principle of hermeneutics is the Bible's *unity*. Hermeneutical reflection has no more important task than to think through the unity of the Bible, to clarify this unity and the way in which it controls interpretation. This is true for all the theological disciplines but clearly so for systematic theology, concerned as it is with providing an explicit statement, under appropriate topics (*loci*), of the teaching of Scripture as a whole.

The church's recognition of the Bible's unity goes back to its beginnings, but the hermeneutical significance of this recognition has been grasped best in the churches of the Reformation. The Protestant Scripture principle *scriptura sola*—it should not be missed—is pointedly hermeneutical; it involves a hermeneutical proposition. So, it is not a detachable or additional principle but brings out and makes explicit the hermeneutical significance of "Scripture alone" when the Reformation and subsequent fidelity to it insist that "Scripture is its own interpreter," "Scripture is the interpreter of Scripture."

This of course does not mean that the Bible is to be understood in isolation, apart from extra-biblical materials insofar as the latter shed light on the background and circumstances in which each biblical book was written. Rather, the thought is that Scripture has a unified sense, a single pervasive meaning, and because of this, it is its own best interpreter, or better, God, its author, is his own best interpreter.

The sense of this self-interpretation has found expression in the often-repeated rule that the more obscure passage is to be interpreted in the light of the more clear, the more difficult in the light of the more easily understood (see Westminster Confession of Faith 1.9 for a classic formulation). This implies that there is a pervasive clarity in the meaning of Scripture, and this clarity is always to be brought to bear upon a specific passage. The unity of Scripture entails its clarity; its unity guarantees this full, unified sense—"the consent of all the parts, the scope of the whole" (Westminster Confession of Faith 1.5).

Expressed otherwise in terms of the principle of context—a principle essential for sound understanding of any text but preeminently and uniquely so for Scripture—every unit of biblical material, however quantified, is qualified by a pattern of contexts relative to itself. Any unit is anchored in an expanding horizon of contexts—like the center of a series of increasingly larger concentric circles—that extends to the Bible as a whole.

To affirm unity and self-interpretation as we have is not at all to overlook that the Bible is marked by all sorts of literary and conceptual variety. Rather, it is *in* this variety or, better, *as* this variety—not in spite of or in tension with it—that there is unity. The unity of the Bible is a unity in diversity. The unity of the Bible consists in the coherence, the concord, the harmony that obtains among a multiplicity of documents involving a variety of literary types and many different human authors. It is in this sense that the unity of Scripture means "the consent of *all the parts*, the scope of the whole" (emphasis added).

Formal and Material Unity

Our comments so far about the Bible's unity have been largely of a formal sort. This has been advisable, even necessary, because so much biblical interpretation today, especially in academic circles, continues to be marked by a more or less self-conscious and forthright rejection of the formal origin and authority of the Bible as God's Word, by a denial that it is God's Word in form as well as content. Assessments of the biblical documents are made from the vantage point of commitment to the rational autonomy of the interpreter ("historical-critical" method). As a result of this approach, the contents of Scripture are distorted and falsified in various ways and its authority relativized and effectively abandoned. Without a controlling commitment to the formal origin and authority of Scripture as God's Word (God as its primary author), its meaning, especially as a whole, becomes obscured and elusive at best.

Adapting here questions posed in Plato's *Euthyphro*, we may ask: (a) is something right/true because it's in the Bible, or is it in the Bible because it's right/true? The answer is "yes." Both are true: (a) something is right and true because it's in the Bible, and (b) it's in the Bible because it's right and true. But proposition (b) can be affirmed—it's in the Bible because it's true—with confidence for the entire Bible, only if proposition (a) is true—because it's in the Bible—that is, because God, the Bible's author, says so. Otherwise, if (a) is denied or not affirmed antecedently, then (b) will necessarily be assessed by standards of what is true and right from outside and above the Bible, standards brought by interpreters and carrying the demand for them to decide what in the Bible may or may not be true or right. For sound interpretation of Scripture, form and content—both ultimately divine in origin—cannot be separated; the formal and the material stand or fall together.

The formal unity of Scripture as God's Word, rightly understood, entails its entire truthfulness and reliability. Its statements do not conflict with each other; what it teaches is not internally contradictory. Doubt about this inhibits proper exegesis. But this does not yet say anything about the unity of Scripture in terms of its specific subject matter, its distinguishing content. Formal unity could plausibly characterize any number of literary formats with their contents. What, then, about the form of the Bible with an eye to its contents, the subject matter that it communicates and that shapes it?

"The Scriptures principally teach what man is to believe concerning God, and what duty God requires of man" (answer to question 3 of the Westminster Shorter Catechism). This statement captures succinctly the doctrinal and moral substance of the Bible's overall teaching. But plainly the Bible is neither a handbook of doctrine nor a manual of ethics (even though it is often treated that way, in practice if not in theory). The Bible, seen in its entirety, is not a theological treatise—a point to which systematic theology, with its particular task, especially needs to remain aware.

The Redemptive-Historical Unity of the Bible

How then should we characterize the unity of the Bible with a view to its subject matter, while also taking into account the various literary genres and multiple human authors that mark it? Is there a way we can do that meaningfully? The positive and appropriate answer to that question lies in recognizing the historical factor involved, specifically, in giving attention to the redemptive (salvation)-historical character of its contents and the revelation-historical nature of its origin.

The opening words of Hebrews (vv. 1–2a) are particularly instructive in this regard since they provide explicit biblical warrant for the approach we are designating redemptive-historical. Along with a couple of other closely correlative references to God's speaking in 2:2–3 and 3:5–6,[2] this assertion both substantiates and facilitates elaborating basic elements in a redemptive-historical, history-of-revelation approach.

---

2. Likewise with God as the explicit or implied subject of forms of the same verb for speaking (*laleō*).

God, having formerly spoken at many times and in various ways to our fathers by the prophets, has in these last days spoken to us in his Son.[3]

This umbrella-like declaration covers all, or at least much, of what the writer goes on to say in the rest of the document. As such, it also provides a sweeping, overarching perspective on God's speech or revelation, a controlling perspective arguably shared, more or less explicitly, by the other New Testament writings. Several interrelated factors may be noted about this statement, reducible to the definitive nuclear assertion, "God has spoken."

First, revelation is in view as a historical phenomenon. Further, revelation has taken place as an ongoing history, a history of revelation that unfolds in two basic stages. The contrast between the old and new covenants prominent later, especially in chapters 8–10, is fairly seen as implicit or anticipated in the two-fold division of 1:1–2a, as well as in 2:2–3 and 3:5–6. The revelation-historical outlook is more specifically a covenant-historical outlook.

Second, God's Son is the consummate and integrating focus of this history. The history of revelation is both complete and a unity. God's having spoken "in the Son" is his "last-days" speaking. Any thought that this speech might be surpassed or superseded is plainly foreign, not only here but everywhere else in the New Testament. God's Son-speech has nothing less than eschatological finality.

The history completed by the Son is also unified in him. Overall Christ-centered unity is particularly clear in 3:5–6.

Now Moses was faithful in all God's house as a servant in testifying to the things that would be spoken, but Christ is faithful over God's house as Son.

---

3. Scripture translations are my own unless otherwise noted.

Here instead of the prophets (1:1) or angels (2:2), Moses stands for the whole of the old covenant, for the law (2:2) as well as the prophets.[4] As such, in his servant capacity "in all God's house,"[5] he is the key witness to "the things that would be spoken," that is, to those future things eventually spoken by God in Christ, God's future last-days speech in the Son.[6] All told, the old covenant functions as a witness that looks forward to and anticipates the new (cf. Luke 24:25–27, 44–47, and many other passages that could be cited). Explicitly, more clearly than in the other two passages, God's revelation in his Son terminates the covenant-historical house-building process as he is its completion. He is the *telos* (cf. Rom 10:4), the goal that gives unity and coherence to the history of revelation in its entirety, old covenant as well as new.

This focus on Christ, at once as comprehensive and completing as it is unifying, shows clearly that the history of post-fall revelation, considered in terms of its subject matter, is in fact the history of *redemption*. God's speech "in the Son" is "salvation . . . spoken through the Lord" (Heb 2:3), with its both realized (cf. 9:26) and still future (9:28) aspects. He embodies, climatically and uniquely, both word (verbal) revelation and deed revelation (cf. John 1:1), with the former interpreting the latter.

Third, this Christ-centered history, complete and unified in its basic two-stage unfolding, is marked by diversity. The diversity of old covenant revelation is accented by the two adverbs translated "at many times" and "in various ways" and by their position as the opening words in verse 1:1 of the Greek text. If, as seems likely, a

---

4. "Moses" (vv. 2, 5) as well as "prophets" (1:1) and perhaps "angels" (2:2) are each plausibly taken as synecdochic, that is, each stands for the whole of the old covenant period, both before and after Moses.

5. Note, *all* he does he does in God's *one*, *single*, *unified* covenant-house-building project in history.

6. Cf. John 5:46, "If you believed Moses, you would believe me, for he wrote about me" (NIV).

distinction is to be made between them, the first has in view different parts or instances (different times and places), the second, different modes and genres.[7]

Whether or not directly within the purview of the text, this emphasis on diversity accommodates and even sponsors the kinds of concerns that have increasingly occupied biblical interpretation in the modern period, but with this basic proviso: for Hebrews (and demonstrably, the other biblical writers), theological and literary interests, on the one hand, and historical interests, on the other, are never competitive or even independent of or indifferent to each other. Genre factors, no doubt semantically significant, as well as essential theological considerations, do not override or supplant but subserve redemptive-historical concerns as those concerns always involve reliable reference to actual historical occurrence. As Geerhardus Vos has memorably put it, "The historical was first, then the theological," and, we may add, "the literary."[8]

The diversity of God's speaking is a function of its taking place "through the prophets." With an eye to the preposition "through" (*en*) we may speak advisedly of the prophets and others as instruments used by God in *his* speaking. Instructive in this regard is the way Hebrews views the activity of Old Testament authors. In Hebrews 4:7, the quotation from Psalm 95 (94 in the Septuagint) is what God (cf. verse 4) is saying "through David," while in Hebrews 3:7 the same quoted material is, without qualification, what "the Holy Spirit says." The Holy Spirit utilizes David such that what David says in the psalm is primarily and more ultimately what the Holy Spirit says. Similarly, elsewhere in Hebrews, in 9:8 both the actual Day of Atonement ritual and the account of it in Exodus and Leviticus seen together (explanatory revelatory word focused on redemptive deed)

---

7. "At many times and in many ways" (esv), "at many times and in various ways" (niv).

8. Geerhardus Vos, *The Pauline Eschatology* (Phillipsburg, NJ: P&R, 1994), 41.

are what "the Holy Spirit indicates." In 10:15, the promise of the
new covenant in Jeremiah 31 is what the Holy Spirit "bears witness
to" and "says." Hebrews, accordingly, plainly supports what amounts
to the classical distinction between God as the primary author of
Scripture and the human writers as secondary authors.

A redemptive-historical orientation requires giving careful attention to this instrumental role of the human authors of the biblical
documents. But that interest is not due to captivation with the "humanity" of Scripture or preoccupation with the limitations of the
human authors at the expense of downplaying or denying Scripture's
primary divine authorship. A concern with revelation as a historical
process should inevitably draw one to the varied human instrumentality that is an integral factor in giving shape to that process. The
distinguishing characteristics and peculiarities of each of the human
authors and what they have written are essential to revelation as historically differentiated. But divine and human authorship, the unity
and diversity of Scripture, are not in conflict. Attention to the writings of the various authors in all their respective individuality and
particularity serves to disclose in its rich diversity the organic unity
and coherence of the Bible as revelation. Nothing in Hebrews suggests that diversity involves conflict or disunity. Every indication is
to the contrary. Particularly chapters 9–10 work out the unity of the
old covenant/new covenant relationship in terms of the *organic* tie
that exists between a type and its antitype, between the shadow and
the reality foreshadowed: Christ, primarily in his identity as (high)
priest.

In summary, the material unity of Scripture, its overall unity in
terms of its content, has no more basic characterization than that
this unity—against the background of the originally "very good" creation (Gen 1:31) and the subsequent entrance of sin in the fall—is
redemptive-historical. The substance of the Bible as a whole is Christ
as the consummate saving revelation of the triune God. In his com-

ing "in the fullness of time" (Gal 4:4), covenant history reaches its nothing less than eschatological culmination. In terms of hermeneutical significance, then, sound interpretation has no more essential task than to consider a text, however factored, within its redemptive- or revelation-historical context.

Systematic Theology and Biblical Theology

The discipline that gives explicit attention to redemptive history in its actual unfolding, and so to the specific contributions made by each of the Bible's human authors in the instrumental role they have within the ongoing history of special revelation, is biblical theology. This raises the question, important hermeneutically, of the difference between biblical theology and systematic theology and how they are related.

Negatively, the difference is *not*, as is too often maintained, that biblical theology considers the Bible purely in terms of its humanity and historically diverse make-up, leaving systematic theology to attend to whatever may be said about its divinely qualified unity. On this understanding the inevitable result is an irremovable tension between divine and human in Scripture, between its unity and its diversity.

Positively, the basic difference between them may be seen in terms of their relationship. Noncompetitive and mutually dependent, biblical theology is the *indispensable servant* of systematic theology. Biblical theology, taking a cue from Hebrews 1:1–2, considers God's speech specifically as it consists in the diverse and historically situated contributions of the various human writers. In doing so, always presupposing the unity of that speech, it serves the more ultimate task of systematic theology to present the overall unified content of that speech, comprehensively, under appropriate headings (God, creation, man, sin, salvation, etc.). To that end, biblical theology is indispensable, simply because, as we have seen, it is indispensable for sound exegesis, the exegesis on which the very existence of systematic theology is staked.

At any one point in actual practice, the relationship between biblical theology and systematic theology is reciprocal. As the systematic theologian is to build on biblical-theological interpretation, so the biblical theologian ought not to operate indifferent to the assessment of the Bible as a whole that systematic theology provides.

This reciprocal relationship may be aptly compared to literary analysis of a great epic drama. Biblical theology is concerned with the redemptive-historical plot as it actually unfolds scene by scene and over time. With an eye to that entire plot, systematic theology considers the roles of the primary actors, God and man. It highlights the constants that mark their characters as well as the dynamics of their ongoing activities and interactions.

As systematic theology builds on biblical theology, as its formulations are informed or, where necessary, reformed by redemptive-historical exegesis, that will serve toward realizing its high calling: to exalt Christ, the one Mediator between God and sinners as he is the final saving revelation of the triune God. Doing that will ensure the soundness and value of the essential contribution systematic theology has to make to the church and its mission in and to the world.

Recommended Reading From Richard B. Gaffin Jr.

"Systematic Theology and Biblical Theology." *Westminster Theological Journal* 38, no. 3 (Spring 1976): 281–299.

"Introduction." In *Redemptive History and Biblical Interpretation: The Shorter Writings of Geerhardus Vos*, edited by Richard B. Gaffin Jr., ix–xxiii. Phillipsburg, NJ: P&R, 2001.

God's Word in Servant Form: Abraham Kuyper and Herman Bavinck on the Doctrine of Scripture. Greenville, SC: Reformed Academic, 2008.

"The Redemptive-Historical View." In *Biblical Hermeneutics: Five Views*, edited by Stanley E. Porter and Beth M. Stovell, 89–110. Downers Grove, IL: IVP Academic, 2012.

APPENDIX A

---⌖---

Westminster Theological Seminary: Its Purpose and Plan

J. GRESHAM MACHEN

Westminster Theological Seminary, which opens its doors today, will hardly be attended by those who seek the plaudits of the world or the plaudits of a worldly church. It can offer for the present no magnificent buildings, no long-established standing in the ecclesiastical or academic world. Why, then, does it open its doors; why does it appeal to the support of Christian men?

The answer is plain. Our new institution is devoted to an unpopular cause; it is devoted to the service of One who is despised and rejected by the world and increasingly belittled by the visible church, the majestic Lord and Savior who is presented to us in the Word of God. From him men are turning away one by one. His sayings are too hard, his deeds of power too strange, his atoning death too great an offense to human pride. But to him, despite all, we hold. No Christ of our own imaginings can ever take his place for us, no mystic Christ whom we seek merely in the hidden depths of our own souls. From all such we turn away ever anew to the blessed written Word and say to the Christ there set forth, the Christ with whom then we have living communion: "Lord, to whom shall we go? Thou hast the words of eternal life" (John 6:68; KJV).

The Bible, then, which testifies of Christ, is the center and core of that with which Westminster Theological Seminary has to do. Very different is the attitude of most theological institutions today. Most seminaries, with greater or lesser clearness and consistency, regard not the Bible alone, or the Bible in any unique sense, but the general phenomenon of religion as being the subject-matter of their course. It is the duty of the theological student, they maintain, to observe various types of religious experience, attested by the Bible considered as a religious classic, but attested also by the religious conditions that prevail today, in order to arrive by a process of comparison at that type of religious experience which is best suited to the needs of the modern man. We believe, on the contrary, that God has been pleased to reveal himself to man and to redeem man once for all from the guilt and power of sin. The record of that revelation and that redemption is contained in the Holy Scriptures, and it is with the Holy Scriptures, and not merely with the human phenomenon of religion, that candidates for the ministry should learn to deal.

There is nothing narrow about such a curriculum; many and varied are the types of intellectual activity that it requires. When you say that God has revealed himself to man, you must in the first place believe that God is and that the God who is is one who can reveal himself, no blind world-force, but a living Person. There we have one great division of the theological course. "Philosophical apologetics" or "theism," it is called. But has this God, who might reveal himself, actually done so in the way recorded in the Scriptures of the Old and New Testaments? In other words, is Christianity true? That question, we think, should not be evaded; and what is more, it need not be evaded by any Christian man. To be a Christian is, we think, a truly reasonable thing; Christianity flourishes not in obscurantist darkness, where objections are ignored, but in the full light of day.

But if the Bible contains a record of revelation and redemption, what in detail does the Bible say? In order to answer that question, it is not sufficient to be a philosopher; by being a philosopher you may perhaps determine, or think you can determine, what the Bible ought to say. But if you are to tell what the Bible does say, you must be able to read the Bible for yourself. And you cannot read the Bible for yourself unless you know the languages in which it was written. We may sometimes be tempted to wish that the Holy Spirit had given us the Word of God in a language better suited to our particular race, in a language that we could easily understand; but in his mysterious wisdom he gave it to us in Hebrew and in Greek. Hence if we want to know the Scriptures, to the study of Greek and Hebrew we must go. I am not sure that it will be ill for our souls. It is poor consecration indeed that is discouraged by a little earnest work, and sad is it for the church if it has only ministers whose preparation for their special calling is of the customary superficial kind.

We are not conducting a school for lay workers at Westminster Theological Seminary (useful though such a school would be), but a theological seminary; and we believe that a theological seminary is an institution of higher learning whose standards should not be inferior to the highest academic standards that anywhere prevail.

If, then, the students of our seminary can read the Bible not merely in translations, but as it was given by the Holy Spirit to the church, then they are prepared to deal intelligently with the question what the Bible means. There we have the great subject of biblical exegesis or biblical interpretation. I hesitate to use that word "interpretation"; for it is a word that has been the custodian of more nonsense, perhaps, than any other word in the English language today. Every generation, it is said, must interpret the Bible and the creeds of the church in its own way. So it is said in effect by many modern leaders of the church: "We accept the Apostles' Creed, but we must interpret the Apostles' Creed in a way that will suit the modern mind. So we repeat the assertion of the Creed. 'The third day he rose again from the dead,' but we interpret that to mean, 'The third day he did not rise again from the dead.'"

In the presence of this modern business of interpreting perfectly plain assertions to mean their exact opposite, do you know what I verily believe? I verily believe that the new Reformation, for which we long, will be like the Reformation of the sixteenth century in that it will mean a return to plain common honesty and common sense. At the end of the middle ages the Bible had become a book with seven seals; it had been covered with the rubbish of the fourfold sense of Scripture and all that. The Reformation brushed that rubbish away. So again today the Bible has been covered with an elaborate business of "interpretation" that is worse in some respects than anything that the middle ages could produce. The new Reformation will brush all that away. There will be a rediscovery of the great Reformation doctrine of the perspicuity of Scripture; men will make the astonishing discovery that the Bible is a plain book addressed to plain men, and that it means exactly what it says.

In our work in exegesis at Westminster Theological Seminary, at any rate, we shall seek to cultivate common sense. But common sense is not so common as is sometimes supposed, and for the cultivation of it true learning is not out of place. What a world of vagaries, what a sad waste of time, could be avoided if men would come into contact with the truly fine exegetical tradition of the Christian church! Such contact with the devout and learned minds of the past would not discourage freshness or originality. Far from it; it would help to shake us out of a rut and lead us into fields of fruitful thinking.

In true biblical exegesis, the Bible must be taken as God has been pleased to give it to the church. And as God has been pleased to give it to the church, it is not a mere textbook of religion written all at one time and in one way. On the contrary, it is composed of sixty-six books written at widely different times and by the instrumentality of widely different men. Let us not regret that fact. If the Bible were a systematic textbook on religion, it would, indeed, possess some advantages: it would presumably be easier to interpret; for much of our present difficulty of interpretation comes from the fact that the biblical books are rooted in historical conditions long gone by. But if the Bible, under those circumstances, would be easier to interpret, it would speak far less powerfully to the heart of man. As it is, God has been very good. He has given us no cold textbook on religion, but a Book that reaches every heart and answers to every need. He has condescended to touch our hearts and arouse our minds by the wonderful variety and beauty of his Book.

When we have learned to read that Book aright, we can trace the history of the revelation that it sets forth. When we do so, we are engaging in an important part of the theological curriculum. "Biblical theology," it is called. Whether it is set forth in a separate course, or whether it is interwoven, as will probably be done in Westminster Theological Seminary, with the work of the Old and New Testament departments, in either case it is a vital part of that with which we have to deal. "God, who at sundry times and in divers manners spake in time past unto the fathers by the prophets, hath in these last days spoken unto us by his Son"—there is the program of biblical theology; it traces the history of revelation through Old and New Testament times.

But biblical theology is not all the theology that will be taught at Westminster Theological Seminary; for systematic theology will be at the very center of the Seminary's course. At that point an error should be avoided: it must not be thought that systematic theology is one whit less biblical than biblical theology is. But it differs from biblical theology in that, standing on the foundation of biblical theology, it seeks to set forth, no longer in the order of the time when it was revealed, but in the order of logical relationships, the grand sum of what God has told us in his Word. There are those who think that systematic theology on the basis of the Bible is impossible; there are those who think that the Bible contains a mere record of human seeking after God and that its teachings are a mass of contradiction which can never be resolved. But to the number of those persons we do not belong. We believe for our part that God has spoken to us in his Word, and that he has given us not merely theology, but a system of theology, a great logically consistent body of truth.

That system of theology, that body of truth, which we find in the Bible is the Reformed faith, the faith commonly called Calvinistic, which is set forth so gloriously in the Confession and Catechisms of the Presbyterian Church. It is sometimes referred to as a "man-made creed." But we do not regard it as such. We regard it, in accordance with our ordination pledge as ministers in the Presbyterian Church, as the creed which God has taught us in his Word. If it is contrary to the Bible, it is false. But we hold that it is not contrary to the Bible, but in accordance with the Bible, and true. We rejoice in the approximations to that body of truth which other systems of theology contain; we rejoice in our Christian fellowship with other evangelical churches; we hope that members of other churches, despite our Calvinism, may be willing to enter into Westminster Theological Seminary as students and to listen to what we may have to say. But we cannot consent to impoverish our message by setting forth less than what we find the Scriptures to contain; and we believe that we shall best serve our fellow Christians, from whatever church they may come, if we set forth not some vague greatest common measure among various creeds, but that great historic faith that has come through Augustine and Calvin to our own Presbyterian Church. Glorious is the heritage of the Reformed faith. God grant that it may go forth to new triumphs even in the present time of unbelief!

Systematic theology, on the basis of Holy Scripture, is the very center of what we have to teach; every other theological department is contributory to that; that department gives a man the message that he has to proclaim. But we have already spoken of the heritage of the

Reformed faith, and of a glorious tradition that has come down to us in the church. And that brings us to speak of another department of the theological curriculum, the department that deals with the history of the Christian church. Our message is based, indeed, directly upon the Bible; we derive the content of it not from the experience of past ages, but from what God has told us in his Word. But it would be a mistake to ignore what past generations, on the basis of God's Word, have thought and said and done. Into many other fields of theological study the study of church history casts a beneficent light. Church history should make us less enthusiastic about a modernity which is really as old as the hills; and amid the difficulties of the present time it should give us new hope. God has brought his church through many perils, and the darkest hour has often preceded the dawn. So it may be in our day. The gospel may yet break forth, sooner than we expect, to bring light and liberty to mankind. But that will be done, unless the lesson of church history is altogether wrong, by the instrumentality, not of theological pacifists who avoid controversy, but of earnest contenders for the faith. God give us men in our time who will stand with Luther and say: "Here I stand, I cannot do otherwise, God help me. Amen."

Thus the minister who goes forth from Westminster Theological Seminary will, we hope, be a man with a message. He will also, we hope, be a man who can so deliver his message as to reach the hearts and minds of men; and to help him do that, the department of homiletics and practical theology has an important place. It cannot, indeed, itself teach a man how to preach; that he must learn, if at all, by the long experience of subsequent years. But at least it can help him to avoid errors and can start him in the right way; it can start him out in that long course in homiletics which is provided by all the rest of life.

Such, very feebly and imperfectly presented, is the program of Westminster Theological Seminary; it is far better set forth in the fine article which Dr. Oswald T. Allis has recently contributed to *The*

Sunday School Times. Many things are omitted from this brief summary of ours. Some of them are omitted because of the imperfections of the speaker or from lack of time. But others are omitted of deliberate purpose. There are many things—many useful things, too—with which a theological seminary should not attempt to deal. Let it never be forgotten that a theological seminary is a school for specialists. We are living in an age of specialization. There are specialists on eyes and specialists on noses, and throats, and stomachs, and feet, and skin; there are specialists on teeth—one set of specialists on putting teeth in, and another set of specialists on pulling teeth out—there are specialists on Shakespeare and specialists on electric wires; there are specialists on Plato and specialists on pipes. Amid all these specialties, we at Westminster Theological Seminary have a specialty which we think, in comparison with these others, is not so very small. Our specialty is found in the Word of God. Specialists in the Bible—that is what Westminster Theological Seminary will endeavor to produce. Please do not forget it; please do not call on us for a product that we are not endeavoring to provide. If you want specialists in social science or in hygiene or even in "religion" (in the vague modern sense), then you must go elsewhere for what you want. But if you want men who know the Bible and know it in something more than a layman's sort of way, then call on us. If we can give you such men, we have succeeded; if we cannot give them to you, we have failed. It is a large contract indeed, a contract far too great for human strength. But at least, by God's grace, we shall do our best.

Such is the task of Westminster Theological Seminary. It is a task that needs especially to be undertaken at the present time. Fifty years ago many colleges and universities and theological seminaries were devoted to the truth of God's Word. But one by one they have drifted away, often with all sorts of professions of orthodoxy on the part of those who were responsible for the change. Until May 1929 one great theological seminary, the Seminary at Princeton, resisted bravely the current of the age. But now that seminary has been made to conform to the general drift. Signers of the Auburn Affirmation, a formal document which declares that acceptance of the virgin birth and of four other basic articles of the Christian faith is nonessential even for ministers, actually sit upon the new governing Board. And they do so apparently with the acquiescence of the rest. Not one word of protest against the outrage involved in their presence has been uttered, so far as I know, by the other members of the Board; and a formal pronouncement, signed by the President of the Seminary and the President of the Board, actually commends the thirty-three members of the Board as men who have the confidence of the church. Surely it is quite clear, in view of that pronouncement, as well as in view of the personnel of the Board, that under such a governing body, Princeton Seminary is lost to the evangelical cause.

At first it might seem to be a great calamity; and sad are the hearts of those Christian men and women throughout the world who love the gospel that the old Princeton proclaimed. We cannot fully understand the ways of God in permitting so great a wrong. Yet good may come even out of a thing so evil as that. Perhaps the evangelical people in the Presbyterian Church were too contented, too confident in material resources; perhaps God has taken away worldly props in order that we may rely more fully upon him; perhaps the pathway of sacrifice may prove to be the pathway of power.

That pathway of sacrifice is the pathway which students and supporters of Westminster Theological Seminary are called upon to tread. For that we can thank God. Because of the sacrifices involved, no doubt many have been deterred from coming to us; they have feared the opposition of the machinery of the church; some of them may have feared, perhaps, to bear fully the reproach of Christ. We do not judge them. But whatever may be said about the students who have not come to us, one thing can certainly be said about those who have come—they are real men.

No, my friends, though Princeton Seminary is dead, the noble tradition of Princeton Seminary is alive. Westminster Theological Seminary will endeavor by God's grace to continue that tradition unimpaired; it will endeavor, not on a foundation of equivocation and compromise, but on an honest foundation of devotion to God's Word, to maintain the same principles that the old Princeton maintained. We believe, first, that the Christian religion, as it is set forth in the Confession of Faith of the Presbyterian Church, is true; we believe, second, that the Christian religion welcomes and is capable of scholarly defense; and we believe, third, that the Christian religion should be proclaimed without fear or favor, and in clear opposition to whatever opposes it, whether within or without the church, as the only way of salvation for lost mankind. On that platform, brethren, we stand. Pray that we may be enabled by God's Spirit to stand firm. Pray that the students who go forth from Westminster Theological Seminary may know Christ as their own Savior and may proclaim to others the gospel of his love.

APPENDIX B

—◈—

Affirmations and Denials Regarding Recent Issues

BOARD OF TRUSTEES

Westminster Theological Seminary is a Reformed seminary that is committed to the infallibility of Scripture and has a well-defined doctrinal basis in the subordinate standards of the Westminster tradition. Each voting faculty member and each member of the Board of the Seminary is required to subscribe to the Westminster Standards, that is, the Westminster Confession of Faith (WCF), the Westminster Larger Catechism (WLC), and the Westminster Shorter Catechism (WSC). Each voting faculty member is required to make the following pledge:

> I do solemnly declare, in the presence of God, and of the
> Trustees and Faculty of this Seminary, that (1) I believe the
> Scriptures of the Old and New Testaments to be the Word of
> God, the only infallible rule of faith and practice; and (2) I
> do solemnly and *ex animo* adopt, receive, and subscribe to the
> Westminster Confession of Faith and Catechisms in the form
> in which they were adopted by this Seminary in the year of our

Lord 1936, as the confession of my faith, or as a summary and just exhibition of that system of doctrine and religious belief, which is contained in Holy Scripture, and therein revealed by God to man for his salvation; and I do solemnly, *ex animo*, profess to receive the fundamental principles of the Presbyterian form of church government, as agreeable to the inspired oracles. And I do solemnly promise and engage not to inculcate, teach, or insinuate anything which shall appear to me to contradict or contravene, either directly or impliedly, any element in that system of doctrine, nor to oppose any of the fundamental principles of that form of church government, while I continue a member of the Faculty in this Seminary. I do further solemnly declare that, being convinced of my sin and misery and of my inability to rescue myself from my lost condition, not only have I assented to the truth of the promises of the Gospel, but also I have received and rest upon Christ and His righteousness for pardon of my sin and for my acceptance as righteous in the sight of God and I do further promise that if at any time I find myself out of accord with any of the fundamentals of this system of doctrine, I will on my own initiative, make known to the Faculty of this institution and, where applicable, my judicatory, the change which has taken place in my views since the assumption of the vow.

Each member of the Board of Trustees subscribes to a similar pledge:

I hereby solemnly declare in the presence of God and this Board (1) that I believe the Scriptures of the Old and New Testaments to be the Word of God, the only infallible rule of faith and practice, (2) that I sincerely receive and adopt

the Confession of Faith and Catechisms of the Presbyterian Church in America in the form which they possessed
in 1936, as containing the system of doctrine taught in the
Holy Scriptures, (3) that, approving the Charter of Westminster Theological Seminary, I will faithfully endeavor to
carry into effect the articles and provisions of said Charter
and to promote the great design of the Seminary. I do further
solemnly declare that, being convinced of my sin and misery
and of my inability to rescue myself from my lost condition
not only have I assented to the truth of the promises of the
Gospel, but also I have received and rest upon Christ and His
righteousness for pardon of my sin and for my acceptance as
righteous in the sight of God.

We continue to embrace the Westminster Standards. We remain
convinced that they are a sound and valuable confessional basis for
the work and instruction in the Seminary.

Theological discussion at Westminster Theological Seminary
has revealed several areas where it may be appropriate for the Board
of the Seminary to reaffirm our continued commitment to the
Westminster Standards and to Presbyterian government, and to re-
state the nature of our commitment. We see the affirmations and
denials below not as an addition to our historic subscription, but as
reaffirmations and clarifications of the implications of our continued subscription.

These affirmations and denials are not in any way exhaustive.
Rather, they are to be seen as selective, and as addressing only some of
the matters implied in confessional subscription. The complete affirmation to which voting faculty members are bound is the faculty pledge,
as quoted above and set out in the Constitution of the Seminary.

Affirmations and Denials

I. Confessional Subscription

A. BASIC CHARACTER OF SUBSCRIPTION

We affirm that the Standards are *subordinate* standards. Scripture itself, as the *primary* standard, is the only infallible rule of faith and practice (see the faculty pledge; WCF 1.2; 1.10; WLC 3; WSC 2).

We deny that the primacy of Scripture makes confessional subscription unimportant or dispensable or superfluous (WCF 22).

We affirm that our subscription to the Standards includes a cordial and full affirmation that the Standards are a just exhibition of the system of doctrine and religious belief which is contained in Holy Scripture (see faculty pledge).

We deny that our subscription merely requires that a faculty member is to be instructed or guided by the Standards.

We affirm that the Westminster Standards are fallible, that is, that it is possible in principle that they may err, and, further, that they are open to revision (WCF 31.4).

We deny that the Westminster Standards are infallible.

B. PROGRESS IN UNDERSTANDING SCRIPTURE

We affirm that Scripture contains truths not included in the Westminster Standards (WCF 1.6).

We deny that there are truths found in Scripture but not in the Standards that overthrow or undermine any element in the system of doctrine expounded in the Standards.

We affirm that God himself enjoins us to seek an ever deeper and more comprehensive understanding of his word (WLC 157).

We deny that we cannot add to or deepen the understanding of God's word expressed in the Standards.

C. Specific Obligations Implied by the Pledge

We affirm that a person who voluntarily pledges subscription to the Standards is bound to keep his pledge (WCF 22; 31.3).

We deny that the Westminster Standards lack binding force on those who subscribe to them.

We affirm that a voting faculty member is not permitted to teach or insinuate something contrary to any element in the system of doctrine, even if the faculty member judges that what he is going to teach is based on Scripture (faculty pledge).

We deny that an alleged Scriptural basis for a teaching eliminates the obligation imposed by the faculty pledge.

We affirm that a faculty member may present to the faculty or the Board an idea that might later be judged out of accord with the system of doctrine, in order to have that idea tested and sifted.

We deny that the confidential presentation of ideas to the faculty or Board for the purpose of testing and evaluation is in itself out of accord with the faculty pledge.

We affirm that individual faculty members may take exception to or express a scruple about a particular item or wording within the Standards.

We deny that taking an exception to a particular item necessarily implies introducing a mental reservation into the faculty pledge, or is necessarily inconsistent with the faculty pledge.

D. Judgments about Subscription

We affirm that, with regard to any exception or scruple, or any other views of a faculty member, the Board and the faculty have a responsibility, both at the time of initial appointment and at all subsequent times, to make a judgment as to whether such an exception or such a view undermines the intent of the Seminary's subscription pledge.

We deny that Board and faculty judgments about compatibility with the Standards constitute an illegitimate interference with an individual's conscience or an illegitimate abridgment of academic freedom.

We affirm that, in the context of subscription by voting faculty and Board members, the meaning of any particular teaching in the Standards is determined by the Board, by referring to the historical record of orthodox Reformed tradition, and is not determined by the private interpretation of any one individual faculty member.

We deny that an individual faculty member has the right to import a private meaning into the Standards when he subscribes, thereby avoiding the meaning commonly understood in the Reformed tradition.

II. Confession and Mission

A. UNIVERSALITY OF TRUTH

We affirm that the truths affirmed in the Standards are true for all times, all places, all languages, and all cultures (WCF 1.1, 6, 8).

We deny that the truths affirmed in the Standards are true only for their seventeenth-century situation or only for some cultures or circumstances.

We affirm that a person's agreement with the content of the Standards includes agreement with all its affirmations as perennially normative, not merely agreement that they were an appropriate response to the theological, ecclesiastical, and pastoral needs of the seventeenth century.

We deny that a person's agreement with the Standards is adequate if, at any point, it merely means agreeing pragmatically with the way in which the Standards addressed the needs of their situation.

We affirm that the Standards have instructional value for all times and all cultures. We deny that the Standards have instructional value only in some cultures.

B. The Legitimacy of Pedagogical Adaptation

We affirm that teaching of the Standards in a particular language or culture can and should take into account the existing previous theological understanding and education, crucial theological and pastoral issues in the circumstances, and problems and opportunities arising in the church and in the surrounding culture (WLC 159).

We deny that theological teaching need not attend to such circumstances.

We affirm that theological teaching can legitimately adjust in teaching style, phraseology, selection of content, use of illustrations, and many other ways that prove significant in facilitating the communication and grasp of truth in the target language and culture (WLC 159).

We deny that adjustments in pedagogy and communicative strategy imply compromise of the truths affirmed in the Standards.

III. Scripture

A. The Inspiration of Scripture

We affirm that the Holy Scripture is to be believed and obeyed, because it is the word of God (WCF 1.4; WLC 157; 160).

We deny that the Holy Scripture is to be believed or obeyed merely because it contains the word of God, or merely because it conveys the word of God, or merely because the Holy Spirit uses it to effect a personal encounter with God.

We affirm that what Scripture says, God says (WCF 1.4; 1.10; 14.2).

We deny that what Scripture says is only sometimes or only partly what God says, or that Scripture only becomes what God says in the act of communication to some person.

We affirm that in causing his word to be written down in the Bible, God, the primary author, used human writers, the secondary authors, often employing them in the full range of their personalities and existing gifts and abilities, with the exception that he kept them from error (WCF 1.2, 4, and proof texts).

We deny that God produced the Scripture without using human authors.

We affirm that God remains true, good, pure, righteous, all-knowing, and immutable when he delivers Scripture to us, and what Scripture says—both in each detail and as a whole—is always consistent with and manifests his character (WCF 1.4; 2.1).

We deny that the presence of human agents in the writing of Scripture, or any other use of means, or any relation to cultural or historical circumstances in the writing, allow the interpreter to dismiss or cease to reckon with the fact that what God says in Scripture is always consistent with his character.

B. THE INTERPRETATION OF SCRIPTURE

We affirm that each verse and passage belongs to a larger context of other Scripture, to which God expects us to attend (WCF 1.2; 1.9; WLC 157).

We deny that any verse or passage can be given its full and proper interpretation by taking it in isolation from the book to which it belongs, or from the Scripture as a whole.

We affirm that we can understand passages of Scripture more deeply when we take into account the historical and cultural circumstances that they addressed (WLC 157).

We deny that historical and cultural circumstances are irrelevant to understanding Scriptural passages.

We affirm that Scripture makes known clearly those things necessary to be believed and observed for salvation, so that even the unlearned may come to sufficient understanding through due use of ordinary means (WCF 1.7).

We deny that extra-biblical knowledge of ancient customs or circumstances is necessary to understand the gospel of salvation in Christ as the central message of Scripture.

C. The Pertinence of Ancient Contexts: Ancient Near Eastern and First Century Mediterranean World

We affirm that God in his wisdom addressed Scripture to his people of long ago in a manner that takes into account their historical setting and their previous knowledge (WCF 7.5; 2.1).

We deny that Scripture fails to take into account the setting of its ancient addressees, or that it fails adequately to address ancient people.

We affirm that what Scripture affirms to its ancient addressees is always true (WCF 2.1).

We deny that limitations in ancient addressees and their setting may ever allow the inclusion of untruths as a part of what Scripture affirms or what it implies.

We affirm that God in producing the canon of Scripture addresses peoples of all subsequent times, places, and cultures (WCF 1.1; 1.8; WLC 155; 156).

We deny that God addresses only the people who lived at the time that a book was written.

We affirm that what the Scripture affirms is to be believed and obeyed by people in all places and cultures (WCF 1.4; 14.2; WLC 156).

We deny that what Scripture affirms lays obligations of belief and obedience only on the original recipients, or only on some cultures.

We affirm that some earlier commands of Scripture have meaning such that their application to our present circumstances must reckon with the changed redemptive-historical conditions in which God addresses us. For example, animal sacrifices that were prescribed in the Old Testament are no longer legitimate now, because Christ has offered the final sacrifice (WCF 19.3, 4).

We deny that there are no commands whose application varies with the changing redemptive-historical context.

D. The Truthfulness of Scripture

We affirm that the Holy Scripture contains a system of doctrine (faculty pledge).

We deny that the Holy Scripture lacks doctrinal unity on any point of doctrine, or that it does not always agree with itself.

We affirm that the Holy Scripture is harmonious in all its teaching (WCF 1.9).

We deny that there are real contradictions in Scripture.

We affirm that Scripture is truthful and without error in what it affirms (WCF 1.4; 2.1).

We deny that Scripture affirms anything that is factually erroneous or is incorrect.

We affirm that Scripture can quote from, allude to, or otherwise represent, in a manner distinct from its own affirmations, the fallible speech and thought deriving from fallible, sinful human beings (e.g., "The fool says in his heart, 'There is no God,'" Ps 14:1).

We deny that Scripture's quotation or representation of fallible thought implies Scripture's own fallibility.

E. THE ROLE OF THE HOLY SPIRIT

We affirm that the work of the Holy Spirit in a person is necessary for that person properly and savingly to understand the Scripture and that full acceptance and a willingness to submit unconditionally to its teaching is essential to such proper understanding (WCF 10.1; 14.2; WLC 104; 155; 157; WSC 89).

We deny that exercise of the rational powers of fallen man is sufficient for a right understanding of Scripture.

We affirm that God's truthfulness and self-consistency belong to what the Scripture says, not merely to what the Holy Spirit may be later alleged to show us through the Scripture (WCF 1.4).

We deny that God's authority belongs only to the Spirit's teaching from the Scripture, rather than to the Scripture itself as well.

IV. Special Areas of Interest

A. SPECIAL AREA: HARMONY OF SCRIPTURE

We affirm that some things in Scripture are difficult to understand, and that we may not always be able easily to explain apparent contradictions (WCF 1.7).

We deny that all parts of Scripture are easy to understand.

We affirm that, through the illumination of the Holy Spirit, we can rightly become convinced from Scripture itself that it is the word of God, even when we do not have an explanation for some of the apparent discrepancies in Scripture (WCF 1.5).

We deny that we must find explanations for each apparent discrepancy before accepting the divine authority of Scripture and submitting to its teaching.

We affirm that each individual passage of Scripture is consistent in its affirmations with every other passage (WCF 1.9).

We deny that passages may contradict one another.

We affirm that when interpreting any passage, the true meaning must be found by comparing the one passage with the rest of Scripture (WCF 1.9).

We deny that it is legitimate to give an interpretation of a passage that is not in harmony with what is affirmed in another passage or passages.

We affirm doctrinal unity and coherence in a given passage between the meaning of God, as its primary author, and the meaning of the human author, however limited may have been the understanding of the latter of what he wrote (WCF 1.4, 5).

We deny that in a given passage the intentions of God and the human writer are doctrinally divergent or discordant.

B. Special Area: Implications of Details in Scripture, Including New Testament Use of the Old Testament

We affirm that we must submit to all that Scripture affirms, not merely to its main points (WCF 1.4; WLC 157; 160).

We deny that the divine authority of Scripture belongs only to its main purpose or only to the main points of its various passages.

We affirm that we must submit to the New Testament affirmations concerning the Old Testament, and not merely to the conclusions that the New Testament draws from them.

We deny that it is ever allowable to submit to conclusions but not to other affirmations in the Scripture. We affirm that the methods and reasoning that Scripture uses in reaching its conclusions are valid. We deny that any Scripture uses invalid methods or reasoning to draw valid conclusions.

C. Special Area: Old Testament Teaching

We affirm that in the Old Testament God spoke to his people in a way that took into account their lack of detailed knowledge of the coming salvation to be revealed in the New Testament (WCF 7.5).

We deny that there are no differences between the Old and New Testaments.

We affirm that what God said in the Old Testament is always in harmony with later teaching in the New Testament, though it may not always be as full or explicit (WCF 7).

We deny that the New Testament shows any contradiction to what is in the Old Testament.

We affirm that we can sometimes understand passages in the Old Testament more deeply in the light of the later revelation that God has given us in Christ (WCF 7.5).

We deny that we can never have more understanding of an Old Testament passage than what was available to people when it was first given.

We affirm that God's intention with respect to an Old Testament passage is consistent with his later reference to or allusion to that passage in the New Testament (WCF 1.9).

We deny that God's intentions at two different points in time, or in two different texts, are ever in disharmony.

We affirm doctrinal continuity and harmony between the original historical and human meaning of an Old Testament text and the meaning a New Testament writer attributes to that text (WCF 1.5; 1.9).

We deny that there is any doctrinal divergence or disparity between the original historical and human meaning of an Old Testament text and its use in the New Testament.

D. SPECIAL AREA: OLD TESTAMENT HISTORY

We affirm that Adam and Eve were real, flesh-and-blood individual human beings and that their fall into sin was subsequent to their creation as the first human beings (WCF 6.1; 7.2; WLC 17).

We deny that the narrative in Genesis 3 is merely symbolic for what is true of mankind in general.

We affirm that God's acts of creation, as listed in each of the six days of Genesis 1, really happened in space and time (WCF 4.1; WLC 15).

We deny that Genesis 1 merely teaches that God made everything.

We affirm that in Genesis 1 God communicated to ancient people in a manner intelligible to them (WCF 1.7).

We deny that Genesis 1 requires special modern knowledge or scientific knowledge for it to be understood.

We affirm that in the Scripture God does not endorse at any point a faulty worldview or cosmology or a faulty aspect thereof (WCF 1.4; 2.1).

We deny that Scripture at any point affirms a faulty cosmology.

We affirm that Noah, Abraham, Isaac, and Jacob were real people who went through the experiences that Genesis describes them as going through (WCF 1.4; 2.1; 14.2; WLC 160).

We deny that the narratives in Genesis about the patriarchs are merely legendary, or that only some smaller core of events really happened.

Westminster Theological Seminary Distinctives

Westminster Theological Seminary defines its distinctive role most basically by its confessional commitment to the Westminster Standards. But we also value the insights that have grown up at Westminster over the decades as the faculty has continued to reflect on the Bible within the doctrinal framework provided by the Standards. We affirm the value of systematic theology in the tradition of John Murray, of biblical theology in the tradition of Geerhardus Vos, of presuppositional apologetics in the tradition of Cornelius Van Til, of biblical counseling in the tradition of Jay Adams, and of missiology in the tradition of Harvie Conn. When rightly done, these programs of investigation and practice build on the truths articulated in the Westminster Standards. The Standards guide us in these disciplines by giving them a sound doctrinal basis. The disciplines show the fruit of the truths of Scripture by applying them to new areas of reflection.

We affirm the value of the disciplines of systematic theology, biblical theology, presuppositional apologetics, biblical counseling, and missiology as these have been practiced at Westminster Seminary.

We deny that these disciplines, when rightly understood and practiced, are in tension with our confessional Standards.

We affirm the importance of conducting these disciplines in conformity with the Standards and the faculty pledge.

We deny that these disciplines need freedom to reach conclusions that may prove to be contrary to the Standards.

We affirm that these disciplines can offer fruitful service both for the church and for growth in understanding of the doctrines of the Standards.

We deny that we have nothing to learn from these disciplines that could deepen or improve our understanding of doctrine.

We affirm that biblical theology (attention to the text in its redemptive-historical context) is the indispensable servant of systematic theology—*indispensable* because it is essential for the sound exegesis on which systematic theology depends, a *servant* because it contributes to the presentation, under appropriate topics, of the teaching of Scripture as a whole and in its overall unity that systematic theology is concerned to provide for the life of the church and its mission in the world.

We deny that biblical theology and systematic theology, properly understood, are in conflict or are alternative approaches to Scripture independent of each other, or that either is dispensable.

We affirm that the teachings of Scripture concerning God,

Christ, man, sin, salvation, and other topics, as those teachings are summarized in systematic theology, offer a sound framework in which to conduct the work of exegesis and biblical theology.

We deny that exegesis or biblical theology can be properly conducted without submission to or in tension with the teaching of Scripture as a whole.

APPENDIX C

―――◆―――

Biblical Theology at Westminster Theological Seminary

RICHARD B. GAFFIN JR.

I have been invited to respond to the observations of D. Clair Davis on the retirement of Professor Douglas J. Green, recently announced by the Board of Trustees of Westminster Theological Seminary.[1] One could respond to these observations at several points. Here I limit myself to addressing just one, clearly central for Dr. Davis.

As Dr. Davis sees things, there is a line initiated by the biblical theological work of Geerhardus Vos that, insofar as Westminster's institutional history is concerned, runs through Edmund Clowney to more recent faculty members who espouse a so-called Christotelic hermeneutical method. This biblical theological line he apparently thinks has been brought to an end by the recent announcement. He laments this outcome deeply, for he perceives it as a great loss for Westminster in what he fears will now be its greatly diminished capacity to serve the church, and so a loss for the church itself as it seeks better understanding of the gospel and greater effectiveness in its ministry to the world (his next to last paragraph).

---

1. See D. Clair Davis's post on World Reformed Fellowship, June 8, 2014; http://westm .in/1O4eAyW.

Clair Davis and I have a long and largely overlapping history with Westminster Theological Seminary. Both of us, former Westminster students, were privileged to serve together on its faculty for an extended period from the mid-1960s until early in the past decade when he retired in 2004 (my own retirement was several years later in 2010—an interval not insignificant for matters occasioning this response). So, I share with Clair the vantage point provided by our lengthy common history from which he assesses the recent events. But I have a decidedly different assessment.

My former colleague believes the decision of the Board of Trustees signals an abandonment of interest in biblical theology and the tradition of redemptive-historical, Christ-centered interpretation, with its fructifying potential for systematic theology and preaching, matters that have been an important and distinctive part of the training provided by Westminster Theological Seminary over the years.

Nothing could be further from the truth. The right and continuing commitment to the role of biblical theology at Westminster Theological Seminary is not in jeopardy. Rather, precisely at issue is whether biblical theology, properly conceived and implemented, will continue at Westminster. What the Board's action reflects is the growing recognition, stemming from the controversy that began to engulf the Seminary around 2006, that at stake are two contending understandings of biblical theology, the one for whom Vos can be said to be the father, the other a more recent and diverging conception, associated with a "Christotelic" interpretation, which, as far as Vos is concerned, understands itself as needing to go "beyond Vos," particularly in his reading of the Old Testament perceived as (too) "flat." The Board through its recent action clearly affirmed the first understanding of biblical theology as taught by Vos and dismissed the second Christotelic version.

At the height of his career, in 1916, Vos wrote:

Reformed theology has with greater earnestness than any
other type of Christian doctrine upheld the principles of the
absoluteness and unchanging identity of truth. It is the most
anti-pragmatic of all forms of Christian teaching. And this is
all the more remarkable since it has from the beginning shown
itself possessed of a true historic sense in the apprehension
of the progressive character of the deliverance of truth. Its
doctrine of the covenants on its historical side represents the
first attempt at constructing a history of revelation and may
justly be considered the precursor of what is at present called
biblical theology. But the Reformed have always insisted upon
it that at no point shall a recognition of the historical delivery
and apprehension of truth be permitted to degenerate into a
relativity of truth. The history remains a history of revelation.
Its total product agrees absolutely in every respect with the
sum of truth as it lies in the eternal mind and purpose of God.
If already the religion of the Old and New Testament church
was identical, while the process of supernatural revelation was
still going on, how much more must the church, since God has
spoken for the last time in His Son, uphold the ideal absoluteness of her faith as guaranteed by its agreement with the Word
of God that abideth forever. It is an unchristian and an un-
biblical procedure to make development superior to revelation
instead of revelation superior to development, to accept belief
and tendencies as true because they represent the spirit of the
time and in a superficial optimism may be regarded as making
for progress. Christian cognition is not an evolution of truth,
but a fallible apprehension of truth which must at each point
be tested by an accessible absolute norm of truth. To take one's

stand upon the infallibility of the Scriptures is an eminently religious act; it honors the supremacy of God in the sphere of truth in the same way as the author of Hebrews does by insisting upon it, notwithstanding all progress, that the Old and the New Testament are the same authoritative speech of God.[2]

Earlier, in his 1894 inaugural address at Princeton Seminary, Vos wrote in a similar vein:

The second point to be emphasized in our treatment of Biblical Theology is that the historical character of the truth is not in any way antithetical to, but throughout subordinated to, its revealed character. Scriptural truth is not absolute, notwithstanding its historic setting; but the historic setting has been employed by God for the very purpose of revealing the truth, the whole truth, and nothing but the truth. It is not the duty of Biblical Theology to seek first the historic features of the Scriptural ideas, and to think that the absolute character of the truth as revealed of God is something secondary to be added thereunto. The reality of revelation should be the supreme factor by which the historic factor is kept under control. With the greatest variety of historical aspects, there can, nevertheless, be no inconsistencies or contradictions in the Word of God.[3]

I certainly do not mean to suggest an exact correspondence between the interpretive approach Vos was opposing in his day and the Christotelic approach approved by Dr. Davis as belonging in the line

---

2. Geerhardus Vos, "Hebrews, the Epistle of the Diatheke," in *Redemptive History and Biblical Interpretation*, ed. Richard B. Gaffin Jr. (Phillipsburg, NJ: P&R, 2001), 232–33.

3. Geerhardus Vos, "The Idea of Biblical Theology as a Science and as a Theological Discipline," in *Redemptive History and Biblical Interpretation*, ed. Richard B. Gaffin Jr. (Phillipsburg, NJ: P&R, 2001), 19.

of Vos. Still, it is difficult to miss an unmistakable affinity between the two approaches. Several observations on the above quotes serve to bring out that similarity.

First, in these passages Vos is concerned with the fundamental and ever-crucial issue of the relationship between revelation and history, between historical development and revealed truth, and specifically how that relationship is to be understood with an eye toward a sound conception of biblical theology.

Noteworthy in that regard is the continuity he sees between his own understanding of biblical theology and "the true historic sense" that has marked Reformed theology from its inception, specifically, covenant theology's awareness of and attention to the historically progressive character of revelation. The epoch-making stature of Vos is not in drawing attention for the first time to the significance of the fundamentally historical nature of revelation, though his work certainly highlights that—especially important where it is missed or underappreciated. Rather, his singular importance is in opening the way, in a post-Enlightenment setting, to biblically sound alternatives in the face of the destructive biblical theologies spawned by the historical-critical method in the late eighteenth and throughout the nineteenth centuries down to his own time. The continuity that Vos sees between his biblical theological work and earlier Reformed theology, then, suggests the need for reconsidering the high grade Dr. Davis assigns to a Christotelic approach at the expense of the Puritans (third paragraph from the end), at least when we consider the best and most able among them (e.g., Owen, Goodwin).

Second, Vos is concerned to stress that within Scripture and the history of revelation (of which the origin of Scripture is a part) the historical character of its truth, while integral, is subordinate to its revealed character. While historical development is essential, revelation, as he says, is "supreme." And that is always so throughout, for "its total product"; "at no point" is that not the case.

It is this point of the entire truthfulness of the history of revelation and Scripture—involving "the truth, the whole truth, and nothing but the truth," as Vos says, and critically essential for any doctrine of Scripture, like that set out in chapter 1 of the Westminster Confession of Faith, intent on doing justice to the unity and coherent harmony of the Bible as God's own written Word—it is just this crucially important point that is compromised or at best obscured by the Christotelic approach to Scripture. This happens through the "first read-second read" treatment of the Old Testament that it adopts. The first read seeks to establish the original historical meaning or original human author meaning of an Old Testament passage on its own terms without any reference to the New Testament. The second read of the passage then seeks to show how in the light of the New Testament it is about Christ, to disclose its Christotelic content.

This approach as a whole is ill-conceived and seriously flawed. Though it is motivated in part by the legitimate concern to avoid reading New Testament meanings back into Old Testament texts— no doubt a danger—there is a difference between reading the New Testament back into the Old and reading the Old Testament in light of the New. The former is wrong; the latter is not only legitimate but also requisite. As it is carried out, the first read tends toward highlighting the "messiness" of the Old Testament, as its proponents put it, toward finding unrelated or discordant trajectories of meaning in the Old Testament. It obscures both the organic connection between the meaning of the divine author and what the human authors wrote, as well as the organic connection and unity between the Old Testament and New Testament.

Multivalent, even contradictory trajectories will appear to be the case when the Old Testament documents are read "on their own terms" in the sense of bracketing out their fulfillment in Christ and the interpretive bearing of the New Testament.

For new covenant readers submissive to both the Old and New Testaments as the Word of God, such a disjunctive reading of the Old Testament is illegitimate, as well as redemptive-historically (and canonically) anachronistic. To seek to interpret the various Old Testament documents for themselves and apart from the vantage point of the New exposes one ultimately to misinterpreting them. The Old Testament is to be read in the light of the New not only because Jesus and the New Testament writers read it this way, but also because Jesus and the New Testament writers are clear about the continuity in intention and meaning that exists between themselves and the various Old Testament authors and what those authors wrote in their own time and place. Passages like Luke 24:44–45, John 5:39–47 and 1 Pet 1:10–12, not to mention numerous others, put this beyond question—unless we are to dismiss such passages, as advocates of Christotelic interpretation characteristically do, as reflecting a Second Temple Jewish hermeneutic that attributes meaning to Old Testament passages that is not their original human author meaning.

The Old Testament reveals a unidirectional path or set of multiple paths that lead to Christ. Certainly at points that way is obscure and difficult to follow; that remains and will always be a challenge to sound interpretation of the Old Testament. Nor did the Old Testament authors grasp with any fullness the meaning of what they wrote. But, as Vos says elsewhere, that they "did not understand all this in detail is not relevant."[4] At the same time, their understanding of what they wrote does not disclose discordant and inorganic discontinuity. As Vos immediately adds, "But without doubt, they would have grasped the heart of the matter." To cite a few examples among many more: "Your father Abraham rejoiced that he would see my day. He saw it and was glad" (John 8:56). "Isaiah said this

---

4. Geerhardus Vos, *Reformed Dogmatics*, ed. and trans. Richard B. Gaffin Jr. (Bellingham, WA: Lexham, 2014), 2:127, on the unity of the covenant of grace.

because he saw Jesus' glory and spoke about him" (John 12:41). Not only did Isaiah speak (or write) but also, in speaking, he himself saw or understood. In fact, with an eye to the syntax of verse 41, he spoke "because he saw"; he said it because he saw it. Again, the intense interest of the Old Testament prophets as a whole was in what "the Spirit of Christ" at work in them was disclosing about his own eventual coming, his sufferings, and consequent glory (1 Pet 1:10–11).

As Vos indicates in the first quote above, at stake here is what is essential for the Reformed faith (e.g., Westminster Confession of Faith 7.5–6; 8.6; 11.6; Westminster Larger Catechism 33–35), for true, biblical religion since the fall: the unity of the religion of the Old and New Testaments focused on Christ. Central for the faith of the former is the future fulfillment of the promise of the Messiah to come; for the faith of the latter, the realized fulfillment of that promise.

Finally, it seems fair to observe that the term "Christotelic" has been coined in part to replace "Christocentric." Advocates of Christotelic interpretation will speak of the Old Testament being "Christological" in a general sense, in view of the pervasive reference to Christ that the New Testament finds in the Old Testament in all its parts. But they avoid applying "Christocentric" to the Old Testament because in their view, their "first read" approach shows that its original historical, human author meaning is, all told, not Christ-centered.

There can be no objection to "Christotelic" in itself. But Scripture is Christotelic just because it is Christocentric. It is Christotelic only as it is Christocentric, and as it is that in every part, the Old Testament included. Or, as we may, in fact must, put the issue here in its most ultimate consideration, Christ is the mediatorial Lord and Savior of redemptive history not only at its end but also from beginning to end. He is not only its omega but also its alpha, and he is and can be its omega only as he is its alpha.

Biblical theology in the tradition of Vos, as it will continue at

Westminster Theological Seminary, Lord willing, seeks to affirm this glorious truth in all its fullness. Biblical theology undertaken as Christotelic interpretation, no doubt despite the best intentions of many of its practitioners, intentions which I commend and honor, nonetheless regrettably obscures and compromises that truth.

From left to right: Iain M. Duguid, G. K. Beale, Richard B. Gaffin Jr., Vern S. Poythress

"I rejoice in the privilege that I have had in teaching hermeneutics at Westminster Theological Seminary for more than thirty-nine years. Our present approach to hermeneutics, as represented by these essays, continues to express what Westminster had stood for from the time of its founding in 1929. At the same time, we are endeavoring to build on the foundation. I commend these essays for expressing a healthy, biblically sound, and doctrinally sound approach, which rests on the infallible Scripture, the very word of God. I hope that such hermeneutics will continue to honor the name of Christ and the divine integrity of Scripture for future generations."

—VERN S. POYTHRESS
Professor of New Testament Interpretation
Westminster Theological Seminary